THE

HAPPY

COOKBOOK

THE HAPPY COOKBOOK

A CELEBRATION OF THE FOOD THAT MAKES AMERICA SMILE

STEVE AND KATHY DOOCY

WM
WILLIAM MORROW
An Imprint of HarperCollins*Publishers*

*This book is dedicated
with love to Peter, Mary, and Sally,
the Original Doocy Test Kitchen.*

CONTENTS

INTRODUCTION

WELCOME TO *THE HAPPY COOKBOOK*

This is not just a cookbook, it's also a book about foods that make people happy.

There's a chance you've picked this up because of the gorgeous portraits of food, and you're right, everything looks so delicious, but as a public service, please don't lick any of the pages until you've paid for the book.

The recipes taste terrific (we've been making them for years) and the instructions are easy and unfussy (we're not too fancy, we don't use a lot of thyme).

My birthday is like Groundhog Day—same cake every time!

Our main goal is for you to understand how certain foods can activate something in the nostalgia department of a person's brain . . . and instantly take them back to a happy place.

Each year on my birthday when my wife, Kathy, re-creates my mom's signature pot roast, as soon as I walk in the front door that smell of it cooking all day transports me immediately fifty years in reverse. I'm ten years old again back in Kansas, doing my homework at our Formica kitchen table as my wonderful mom shakes the Lipton onion soup over that *same* pot roast. Elvis is belting out a classic on the living room Magnavox and all is right with the world.

The simple *smell* of a pot roast can do that, because most of us are blessed with the ability to remember things with our noses.

But it's not just an aroma that can trigger a smile, it can be something random. You won't understand this until you've read the cookbook . . . but whenever I open a car trunk, I think of our wedding cake.

If I see the word *bourbon*, I'll recall the White House official who bakes with a hammer.

And when I hear the word *mahi-mahi* I'm back on our Hawaiian honeymoon after three days of not speaking to each other—that by the end of the trip we were giggling about, thanks to a miraculous invention called wine.

Every one of these hundred-plus recipes makes somebody smile, so there's a story that explains that at the beginning of every recipe. Some have profound reasons, others don't have a cosmic connection, they are simply things that make somebody feel good on the inside.

Because Kathy and I have been married for over thirty years, many of these dishes arrived in our lives accidentally; from our dental hygienist, a flight attendant who washed her hands with vodka in the pre-Purel days, the 4-H club, the back of a soup can, a scene in a Nancy Meyers movie, a church cookbook, a colonial kitchen, a daughter's boyfriend, *two* White House press secretaries, a very famous rock star, a very famous golfer, a TV sitcom director, an honest-to-goodness American hero, and, of course, our family.

Here's the best news for you: Sometimes just being reminded about something sublime is enough to tide you over until you have the real thing again. You've got your own lifetime of experiences to rewind, so are you ready to read our stories and make our foods and see if they jog your memory? If so, soon you'll see a car trunk and also think *wedding cake*.

Besides, what do you have to lose? As Erma Bombeck once said, "Seize the moment. Remember all those women on the *Titanic* who waved off the dessert cart."

Most of us go through life eating three meals a day. Starting now, try to make at least one of them happy.

Enjoy!

Steve Doocy

APPETIZERS

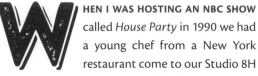 **HEN I WAS HOSTING AN NBC SHOW** called *House Party* in 1990 we had a young chef from a New York restaurant come to our Studio 8H at 30 Rock and prepare one of his favorite recipes on TV. It was so clever and delicious that when he invited Kathy and me to his restaurant for her birthday, we jumped at the offer. It was decades before OpenTable, and I was never good at planning ahead, and it might be free!

When we got there we quickly spotted half a dozen boldface names from Page Six. Everybody looked rich and famous—and actually, most probably were. We were parked momentarily at the bar next to William F. Buckley and his wife, Pat. Both had highballs in hand as they were glamming it up with a couple who looked like they had a cul-de-sac named after them in Greenwich.

The maître d' soon seated us at a table for two next to Frank and Kathie Lee Gifford, whom we'd seen on TV for years but never met, and it was really awkward, because my TV show aired at 9 a.m. weekdays opposite her show, *Regis and Kathie Lee*, and they were killing us in the Nielsens. Taking the high road, I introduced the Doocys to the Giffords, and they could not have been nicer, but I am 100 percent positive they thought we were tourists from Akron just living it up in Fancy Town.

Then that unknown chef who invited us to his restaurant came over to chat. We had never heard of him thirty years ago when he was the executive chef of New York's original Le Cirque, but today Daniel Boulud is a restaurant rock star and one of the greatest chefs in the world. We met him when he was just getting started on his meteoric journey. It's that same feeling of satisfaction one might have if they'd bought Amazon stock at $8.

The future-famous Mr. Boulud came out midway through our first adult beverage and told us that the reason we'd not been shown the menu was that he was making us dinner himself—we should just sit back, relax, and enjoy whatever came through the kitchen door. But first he asked us what we didn't like. Kathy said she loved everything. My dislikes? Tetanus shots and ABBA. Bad joke—it was probably the foie gras talking. I don't know how my joke translated into French, but I believe that no ABBA was harmed in the production of my meal.

Had Instagram been invented in 1990, I would have shocked the room and taken pictures of the five courses. There were cheeses and caviar, and things were sautéed, flambéed, and poached to perfection. Adorable petite portions meant we'd have room for a showstopping filet served with a sauce I'm planning on having every day in Heaven. After a bottle of Champagne and a bottle of Chardonnay, Daniel sent over the ultimate New York dessert: a jaw-dropping three-foot-high spun-sugar and chocolate rabbit cake roughly the size of Selena Gomez.

Meanwhile, Kathie Lee and Frank finished their sponge cake.

It was official: In perhaps the coolest dining room in the Big Apple, a lot of those jaded New Yorkers looking our way seemed a little pea-green jealous. Perhaps they wondered, "Who is *that* guy, and why does his wife get the big bunny birthday cake?"

In fact it was Kathy's thirtieth birthday. But when it was time to present her with a gift I apologetically told her I'd been really busy at work trying to beat *Regis and Kathie Lee* (Kathie Lee stopped talking to Frank to listen) and hadn't had time to go shopping. I handed her a card. Inside was a personal check for $75. The memo line said, "Happy Birthday, Kathy!"

Clearly this was a joke amount; a spouse's thirtieth birthday should be worth closer to $150. I thought it was hilarious, until she started crying. The Giffords were suddenly in no hurry to get their car—who knows what might happen next with the couple from Akron?

You know that flop sweat you get when you realize you've made a terrible miscalculation? I was having some of that. I quickly told Kathy I had one more thing for her, and she stopped streaking her mascara long enough to open a little red box wrapped in white ribbon. Inside was an exact replica of the sapphire and diamond earrings she'd loved on Princess Diana. I'd called her friend Buzzy in the Diamond District and he'd made them especially for Kathy. With that, she was crying again, but these were the good kind of tears.

The Giffords smiled and said goodnight and happy birthday to Kathy. Thus concluded the greatest meal of our lives, which we still talk about thirty years later.

Greatest meal, yes—but it wasn't the *happiest* meal. That meal happens every year in mid-October, when Kathy browns a four-pound chuck roast and puts it in a Dutch oven with dry Lipton onion soup mix and a can of Campbell's cream of mushroom soup—the same pot roast my mom made for me for every birthday of my youth after about the age of eight. As soon as I walk through the door and smell that pot roast, I'm suddenly transported back to a simpler time, before life got complicated and our family scattered across the map.

Now having been married for over thirty years, Kathy doesn't even have to ask what I want for my birthday meal. She knows I want my mom's pot roast and a German chocolate cake—the same cake I always asked my mom to make on my birth-

Kathy's version of my mom's cake takes me back. . . .

Mmmmmm. . . . Mary loves pizza in Rome.

day. Today Kathy bakes it first thing every October 19, and it always makes me happy, because it reminds me of my childhood and my family.

Back then, in Kansas, I thought *German* chocolate sounded so exotic, and it wasn't until we started writing this cookbook that I discovered it's not from Germany at all; the baker who invented dark baking chocolate was named Samuel German. For over fifty years, I'd assumed my favorite cake was from Germany. Nope.

#FakeCakeNews

I also just discovered that National German Chocolate Cake Day is June 11, my mother and father's anniversary . . . what a coincidence.

When we commenced writing this cookbook, I started asking people what their happy meal was, and everybody knew exactly what I was talking about.

"German chocolate cake . . ." Dr. Mehmet Oz said with a big grin.

"I love that, too!" I exclaimed. Then I wondered, if that's his favorite food, what's his cholesterol number?

". . . but that's for my birthday," he said, adding, "For holidays, I also love [wife] Lisa's sweet potatoes with pomegranates."

He's got two favorites? Turns out, most of us have lots of different dishes that activate something in the nostalgia department of our brains.

"There's nothing better than the smell of food cooking," Pioneer Woman Ree Drummond told me on *Fox & Friends*. "That smell when you're walking in the door and your house smells like a roast—it reminds you of your childhood." Exactly!

Stuart Varney, the famous business television host, has a food that takes him back to his happy British childhood. "When I was a youngster living at home with my parents, my favorite dish was roast pork with all the trimmings," he told me. "That is, a pork roast with 'crackling'—that's when the skin is super-cooked until it is crispy." Stuart also tells me that he loves overcooked vegetables like Brussels sprouts, roast potatoes, store-bought applesauce, and, most important, gravy. English cuisine, Stuart says, "requires lubrication." I don't know what that means exactly, and I was too polite to ask.

When Stuart said the pork skin was baked to a crisp and the vegetables were overcooked, I was skeptical that someone would love pork *that* crazy-crunchy on the outside, but then famed Australian golfer Greg Norman mentioned that his favorite dish is exactly the same thing: crackling pork roast.

"The Sunday roast was a feature of my life in Britain," Stuart added. "It's not necessarily healthy for you, but it tasted just right. And if that's what you are brought up on, that's what you like."

He's absolutely right.

Then there are the people who are far away from home, like those serving in the US military. Ever wonder what they're thinking about when they're in a combat zone waiting for somebody to start shooting at them?

Chicken and noodles.

That's what does it for Major Dan Rooney, USAF, a fighter pilot who flew many missions over Iraq. When he's deployed, in quiet moments he thinks about what it will be like when he finally gets to go back home to Owasso, Oklahoma, where he'll open that front door, smell the dinner made by his wife, Jacqy, get an almost Heimlich hug from his girls, and whatever hell he's been through in the last couple of months just melts away.

"I think we all have recipes in our lives that have emotion attached to them," Dan told me, "and chicken and noodles was always a *coming home* recipe from my three tours of duty in Iraq. It's that safe thing—you smell it and it makes you feel good. You get to sit down and eat something that makes you feel good, and the world goes away."

Sometimes just thinking about a beloved dish from your past is enough to tide you over until you can have the real thing again. That's why we decided to write a book filled with favorite recipes that make people happy.

Now, don't worry—this book isn't about Stuart Varney's overcooked vegetables. Most of these dishes are classic recipes that everybody likes, and each has a story that explains what makes it special for someone.

This cookbook is a collection of recipes curated over a lifetime. Because some of the dishes were originally created by our moms, who never wrote down their recipes, we've spent the better part of thirty years trying to re-create that taste of home, and it's a privilege to set them down here for future generations.

That's also one of the reasons we wanted to write this cookbook. The year before we started this project, Kathy was diagnosed with ocular melanoma, an unbelievably rare and aggressive form of eye cancer. She was lucky that they caught it early and she was treated by Dr. Carol Shields and her team of specialists at the Wills Eye Hospital in Philadelphia. During her very first examination, Dr. Shields told Kathy, "I am going to save your life," and she did.

During her recovery, while taking stock of her life as many do when they've gone through something that life-changing, Kathy vowed to make it her personal quest to leave her children a written record of the foods they grew up loving. They don't cook much now, but they will someday.

This pimiento cheese is a grate recipe.

This will always be part of Kathy's legacy to Peter, Mary, and Sally, that wherever they travel in their lives, they'll always have a printed road map to their mom's signature suppers, provided they will want to actually cook and not order takeout on Uber Eats.

What qualifies us to write a cookbook? My grandma Lillian was a professional cook, my sister Ann owned a restaurant and ran a catering business, and I hate to brag, but when I was a kid in 4-H I did win a blue ribbon at the Kansas State Fair for my chocolate chip cookies. Family recipe? Nope, it was printed on the side of the yellow chocolate chip bag. Lesson learned: Don't mess with perfect.

And I don't want to toot my own horn—but I was on Food Network years before Ree, Bobby, Guy, Giada, and Trisha. It was a New York–based show called *Ready, Set, Cook!*, and the plot was simple: Cook a meal in half an hour and try not to cut your finger off. All I remember is at the end they gave me a T-shirt that I wore to various events, hoping somebody would say, "Hey, didn't you make a veal scaloppine in half an hour on Food Network?," to which I'd nod and wave a hand with all my fingers intact. I'm still waiting for someone to mention that. Would somebody please add it to my Wikipedia page? Thank you.

But the most consequential training I got was thanks to my TV jobs. By now I've conducted hundreds of cooking segments with famous chefs and food personalities who came on TV to sell their cookbooks, pans, diets, or cutlery. Every cooking segment has been pretty much the same: introduce them, then they throw some ingredients in a hot saucepan and ask me to stir as they pitch their products. I'm not a sous-chef, but I've played one

On Thanksgiving we're all smiles before someone gets stuck with the dishes.

on TV to the world's greatest cooks. I've stirred with Daniel Boulud (you knew that), and also Julia Child, Gordon Ramsay, Wolfgang Puck, Emeril Lagasse, Bobby Flay, Rachael Ray, Paula Deen, Jacques Pépin, Guy Fieri, Nobu Matsuhisa, Todd English, Martha Stewart (before prison), and Martha Stewart (after prison).

As for Kathy's credentials? On one of our first dates I thought she'd made a delicious meal, but it wasn't until years later that I learned the truth: The day she made me that lasagna was the first time she'd ever turned on her apartment's oven. A single girl in her late twenties, she knew that the fastest way to a man's heart was through his gut, so she'd found a recipe in the Betty Crocker cookbook and started cooking. A kitchen ingenue with little experience, she faked her way through the recipe, and thirty minutes into it the oven caught fire. Then of course the smoke alarm wouldn't turn off, so she removed it from the ceiling and tried to take the battery out. It had a sealed power supply, so she went to the parking lot, threw it in her Jetta and returned to the kitchen to try to salvage the lasagna.

A quirk of Kathy's back then—and today—is that if a recipe calls for one pound of something, she'll buy two, so she has the backup ingredients handy, plus *all* the mozzarella (since she'd forgotten to put any cheese in the original). It was ultimately the best Italian meal I'd ever had. Okay, it *might* have been great, or it *could* have been the wine, or then again maybe I just wanted to kiss the cook.

What was it about that first lasagna that prompted me to essentially propose at the end of our first date? Please don't think this is weird, but it could have been the cheese.

New Year's Eve flute practice.

MY MOM MADE A GREAT LASAGNA, BUT IN THE SEVENties Kansas home cooks didn't use mozzarella or shredded cheese; they used cottage cheese. So when Kathy broke out the ricotta, it was love at first bite.

We got married within the year. Fast-forward about a dozen years and she was a pretty good cook. Then, thanks to our dog, Charlie, she became a *really* good cook.

Please don't imagine we had a talking dog, classically trained at the Cordon Bleu, who showed her how to truss a chicken. Come on—dogs can't truss anything; they don't have thumbs! No, a very excited Charlie knocked Kathy over in the driveway, breaking her kneecap. She would go on to have four surgeries that did not work and one total knee replacement that did. On doctor's orders, she couldn't stand or walk, so she spent hundreds of hours flat on her back on the living room couch watching Food Network.

Ready. Set. Heal!

Kathy learned how to cook. Her mom never taught her—the TV did.

She got really excited thinking about what she would do in the kitchen when she was back on her feet and started a list of the first meals she'd prepare when she was given the green light to return to normal life.

"I can't wait to make a balsamic reduction sauce," she told me more than once as I nodded, thinking, *Does she mean gravy?*

There was a downside to her graduate degree in Food TV, of course. Kathy was coming off a very serious bone surgery, and the only way to control the pain was with pain pills, which she reluctantly took. One day the FedEx delivery guy knocked on our door with a six-foot-long box from QVC.

"Weird . . . I've never watched that channel."

Apparently a week earlier, she'd taken a pain pill and then probably fallen asleep, awoken in the middle of the night, started channel surfing, and stopped to watch Chuck Norris talk about how his Total Gym would change your life. Guess what showed up at our house?

We could have called and told them we didn't mean to order it, but would you ask Chuck Norris for a refund after a medically sedated family member called a TV show? Of course not. So we kept the Total Gym, and it's still in the box in our basement, next to the box containing the NordicTrack.

Side note—Kathy and I wrote *The Mr. & Mrs. Happy Handbook* so that I could keep her company while she rehabbed her bionic kneecap. For months I'd race home after work to make her meals and get her groomed and fed as we chronicled the funny parts of getting hitched and having kids.

Eventually Kathy recovered and returned to the kitchen. She now loves to show off her bal-samic reduction sauce and is hands down the best cook I know. All that Food Network watching paid off—in fact, the idea that we write a cookbook was 100 percent Kathy's. I thought it was a great idea, but there are so many different kinds of cookbooks. What would be the theme of ours?

Kathy wondered, "Is there any way we could work in *The Mr. & Mrs. Happy Handbook*?"

We'd already done a happy book, so at first I thought it was a dumb idea, but ten seconds after she said it, I did this in my head:

HAPPY HANDBOOK + COOKBOOK =
HAPPY COOKBOOK

And she thinks I never listen to her!

And that's where the idea was born. Because every one of us has particular food memories that make us happy, and this book is our chance to celebrate and share them.

I was on a Delta flight once and got upgraded to first class, and when given the choice between the turkey panini or the chicken salad, I chose the sandwich, which was served with a dessert. As soon as I saw it, I had a flashback to my father, Jim.

It was a tiny tiramisu. Sometimes it's hard to tell what airline food is, but tiramisu is easy, with its telltale cocoa powder dusted on top.

I thought of my dad because one time he visited us in New Jersey and Kathy, knowing how much he loves dessert, picked up something we'd never tried before: a frozen Costco tiramisu. Dad loved it and said he wanted to buy it back home in Abilene, Kansas. We looked for the closest Costco to his house and it was too far, so Kathy promised to send him one whenever he wanted it. The tiramisu was $14, but the shipping was $45, plus the dry ice and Styrofoam. It was an ambitious gesture, but my father loved it, so it was worth it.

Seeing that shooter-size tiramisu on my tray made me stop and smile before I ate every bit. Delta's version was not as creamy as Costco's, but because of the memories, it was every bit as sweet.

So, will you find your own happiness in these hundred-plus recipes? We hope so—we chose them because many people already have. The dishes in this book are mostly American classics that everybody loves. Some have been adapted over the years to keep our kids interested in coming home, and others were given to us by some very famous people, friends of ours who shared recipes that simply make them happy.

And it's not just the food—you'll read about the happy memories and stories that accompany these family favorites.

My mom used to keep about a half dozen menus propped up on a shelf in the hall closet. They were quite ornate; I remember one of them had black velvet on the cover, with the restaurant name in gold. I asked one day why we had these menus, and Mom explained that when she and my dad were on their honeymoon in the Wisconsin Dells, wherever they went, they either asked the waiter if they could keep a menu as a souvenir, or they simply took it. They didn't have much extra money for mementos, but they wanted something they could bring home that would always remind them of the most magical week of their lives.

That made sense, because more than once I saw Mom looking for something in the closet, and she'd glance at one of the menus, and I'd notice she'd have a hint of a smile, as she was transported back to the first week of what would be a forty-some-year marriage. It looked to me like she was pondering ordering lunch, but to her it was a time machine to a happy place.

We all have treasured recipes we've collected over the years that eventually become part of the fabric of our lives. That casserole you always take over to a friend who needs cheering up, or that tray of ziti you delivered to your neighbors who just had a new baby girl. The meal your kids begged you to make when they came home from college, or the recipe from that place with the velvet menu where you ate on your honeymoon—all remind you of something good.

So you won't be confused, Kathy is the genius behind the recipes, while all the stories are written from my point of view. Really I'm just reporting from our dinner table, with stories that are as common to other American families as our own. As in your house, there's randomness in how these become favorites. Sometimes you're not just making a meal; you're making a memory.

But let's be clear—you can't just throw a blob of stuff on a plate and expect it to be a crowd-pleaser. You want those memories to be good!

A very famous former celebrity real estate-developer-turned-president whose happiest two foods are #1, hamburgers, and #2, meatloaf, might call finding family favorites what it truly is: *the art of the meal.*

BEST BURRATA BALL

Hate to name-drop, but Tiger Woods made this appetizer for us.

Okay, that sounds as if the golfer put on an apron and made it himself—and it was supposed to. In reality, we ordered his version off the menu at Tiger's restaurant, called The Woods Jupiter. Now we make our own creation any time we have the deep-fryer plugged in and are flash-frying things. The combination of the bread crumbs on the outside and the creamy burrata on the inside is simply splendid.

As Voltaire once observed, "The family that eats fried cheese together is a happy family."

Did I say Voltaire? I meant Fablo.

Canola oil, for deep-frying
1½ cups flour
1 large egg
¾ cup milk
1½ cups plain dried bread crumbs
Four 4-ounce burrata balls
1½ cups your favorite marinara, warmed
Grated Parmesan cheese, for garnish
Shredded basil leaves, for garnish
Toasted sliced baguette, for serving
    (optional)

1. Heat the oil in a deep-fat fryer to 375°F.

2. Set out three shallow bowls or plates. Place the flour in one, whisk the egg and milk in the second until smooth, and put the bread crumbs in the third.

3. Roll a burrata ball in the flour to coat it well, then coat it completely in the egg/milk mixture, then roll it in the bread crumbs so every spot is covered. Now let's give it one more layer, so coat it again in the egg/milk and then back in the bread crumbs. Set aside and repeat with the other burrata balls.

4. Carefully place the balls in the fryer and fry until golden brown, about 5 minutes. Keep an eye on them because they do start leaking. Place the fried burrata balls on paper towels to soak up any grease.

5. On either a communal serving platter or individual saucer, create a little pool of marinara, then place the hot burrata ball in the sauce. Garnish with Parmesan and a pinch of shredded basil. You can then either cut up and eat the burrata with a fork or serve it with toasted bread.

GREEN EGGS AND HAM POTATOES

When our son, Peter, was thirty he finally confessed why he wouldn't touch the deviled eggs Kathy had made at family holidays. "I don't like the squishy white part of the egg... any egg."

But Kathy and I always *loved* deviled eggs even if our kids didn't, so we'd do our best to disguise them. We started making deviled eggs out of fresh avocados, replacing the yellow part of the deviled eggs with something pretty close to guacamole, but Peter was adamant. "Dad, the squishy white part of the egg is still freaking me out...."

One night we had boiled new potatoes on the table, and in a moment of inspiration somebody suggested we spoon out some potato and spoon in the green stuff. Suddenly we had something that resembled a green deviled egg made out of a potato. "Try this, Peter...." He ate five.

Today we toss on some bacon or ham bits, and on Dr. Seuss Day we make what the kids would not taste twenty years ago: green eggs and ham. And kids love them! After all, really they're just potatoes and something like guacamole.

"I really like green eggs and ham. I really like them, Steve-I-Am."

Salt
1 pound small white new potatoes (at least a dozen), well scrubbed
4 large eggs
2 teaspoons fresh lime or lemon juice
2 tablespoons mayonnaise (Duke's is our favorite)
1 tablespoon sour cream
1 teaspoon Dijon mustard
Freshly ground black pepper
1 avocado
3 slices bacon, cooked, chopped into small pieces

1. Bring a medium saucepan of salted water to a boil. Add the potatoes and cook until they are potato salad–tender, 12 to 15 minutes. Set aside to cool.

2. Meanwhile, put the eggs in a saucepan and fill with salted water to about 1 inch above the eggs. Bring to a boil over high heat and cook for about a minute, then cover, remove from the heat, and let sit for 12 minutes. Let the eggs cool a bit, then remove and discard the shells.

3. Halve the hard-boiled eggs lengthwise, as you would for deviled eggs. Place the yolks in a food processor and discard the egg whites (or eat them!). Add the lime juice, mayo, sour

cream, mustard, ½ teaspoon salt, and ¼ teaspoon pepper. Slice the avocado in half, remove the pit, and scoop the avocado into the food processor. Process until the mixture is super smooth, then give it a taste and add more salt and pepper to taste. Set aside.

4. Halve the potatoes lengthwise. Using a melon baller, scoop out a hole in each potato to make it resemble the white part of a deviled egg. Set the potato halves on a serving tray as you go.

5. Scoop up to a tablespoon of the avocado mixture into each of the potato halves.

6. Sprinkle the tops with the crumbled bacon bits. You can serve them immediately or refrigerate until ready. Voilà—green eggs and ham!

MARTHA'S ARTICHOKE DIP

· MAKES 8 SERVINGS ·

When Martha Hockman, one of our oldest family friends, would visit us, she'd ask, "Can I bring anything?"

The answer was always "*Yes, that artichoke thing!*"

The secret ingredient that makes it so fantastic? *Hot mayo.*

Today we keep a couple cans of artichokes and chilies in the cupboard just in case somebody stops by and we want to impress them by making them think we've been cooking all afternoon.

The problem with this recipe is not how it tastes; it's who you invite to eat it. This is all about trust, because you want somebody who won't double-dip. I have accused many a child of double-dipping, to which they always respond, "I'm using the other end of the cracker, Dad." Seems reasonable, but just know who you invite into your hot mayo dip. You don't want to get paranoid about that guest with the sniffles. Am I right?

Two 14-ounce cans artichoke hearts, drained
Two 4-ounce cans diced green chilies
1 cup high-quality mayonnaise (Duke's is our favorite)
2 cups + 2 tablespoons grated Parmesan cheese
Paprika, for garnish
Crackers, for serving

1. Preheat the oven to 350°F

2. In a large bowl, combine the artichokes, chilies, mayo, and 2 cups Parmesan. Mix thoroughly, then transfer the mixture to an 8 x 8-inch baking pan. Sprinkle with the remaining 2 tablespoons Parm and a couple shakes of paprika.

3. Bake until the top is golden brown, 30 to 40 minutes.

4. Serve warm with your favorite dipping crackers.

PIMIENTO CHEESE DIP

If you go to our refrigerator right now, there will be three kinds of pimiento cheese spread, because we fell in love with it during our annual trips to Sea Island in Georgia and Palmetto Bluff in South Carolina. People love it so much they've given it charming nicknames, including *Carolina Caviar*.

Paula Deen, the cookbook queen of Savannah, gave us one cardinal rule when it comes to making pimiento cheese. She told me, "Don't buy the pre-shredded cheese from the store; shred it yourself. And one more thing—don't shred it finely. Go coarse."

Of *coarse*, Paula, that's *grate* advice.

I'll be here all week, try the veal. Kidding, try this pimiento cheese.

P.S. This makes a great sandwich. They spread a similar recipe on two pieces of white bread at the Masters in Augusta, Georgia. By the way, the cost of a four-day badge to the 2018 Masters is in the thousands of dollars. Cost at the Masters for one of their famous pimiento cheese sandwiches? $1.50.

1 cup mayonnaise (Duke's is our favorite)
One 4-ounce jar diced pimientos, drained
1 teaspoon Worcestershire sauce
¼ teaspoon red pepper flakes
1 jalapeño pepper, seeded and minced
1 teaspoon finely grated green onion (white part only)
Salt and freshly ground black pepper
1 pound extra-sharp Cheddar cheese, coarsely shredded

We used to mix all the ingredients at once, but Paula also told us to mix everything *but* the cheese first to get it nice and smooth, then adjust the taste with salt and black pepper the way you like it, and *then* add the cheese. Give it a good stir, refrigerate at least 1 hour, serve, and savor. We've heard people say this will keep for a week or two if stored in an airtight container in your refrigerator. We wouldn't know; it's always gone the second day.

ENCINO MOM'S GUACAMOLE

When Kathy was growing up in Encino, California, across the street from Roy Rogers (the TV star, not the restaurant), there were avocado and orange trees in her backyard. She and her brothers would happily pick, peel, and eat the fruit of both trees, which meant that, unlike many storybook pirates, they never got scurvy.

Kathy started making this recipe when she was twelve years old! Of course you can jazz it up with jalapeños, garlic, sour cream—practically anything, and we have, but we always come back to her original recipe, her heirloom guac, which one of our kids calls *guac-a-mommy*.

4 avocados, pitted and scooped out
2 Roma (plum) tomatoes, seeded and finely diced
¼ cup finely diced red onion
Juice of 1 lime
2 tablespoons finely chopped cilantro leaves
Salt and freshly ground black pepper
Tortilla chips, for serving

1. In a medium bowl, mash the avocados with a fork until smooth.
2. Mix in the tomatoes, onion, lime juice, and cilantro. Season with salt and pepper to make it how you like it. You're done!
3. Serve with your family's favorite tortilla chips.

QUEEN OF CABLE'S QUESO

•MAKES 30 SERVINGS•

We have had Dana Perino and her husband, Peter, over for dinner, and there's no couple we've ever met who have such great stories about their incredible lives. Ask Dana sometime about the time she and her former boss, George W. Bush, called Vladimir Putin on the red phone and pretended it was Tony Blair looking for Putin to cosign a home equity loan. The hilarity ensued.

When I asked Dana about the meal that made her happy, she mentioned a dish with an odd name that I could not locate, but her description sounded exactly like my mom's bierock recipe (which I was already including in the book), so I asked for her second favorite. Turns out that was an easy question. Dana had hosted a queso cook-off contest at her apartment for the entire staff and hosts of *The Five*. She challenged the show's executive producer.

By the end of the judging, Dana won. When asked whether there was a prize, Dana said, "Yes . . . bragging rights."

I have been a connoisseur of queso going way back to college, and when I got married, I naturally tried to convince Kathy that molten Velveeta was a thing of beauty. But she was a cheese snob and the first time she made a similar recipe, she used Cheddar in place of the cheese in the yellow box. It was terrible. When she consented to make it with Velveeta, it was divine.

Dana's cable queso recipe is even more divine—double divine, if that's possible. Every NFL team should require somebody to make this recipe at every tailgate, because this would be good for football.

> One 32-ounce package Velveeta (or fondue cheese), cubed small
> Two 10-ounce cans Ro-tel tomatoes with chilies
> One 10-ounce can cream of mushroom soup
> 1 pound lean ground beef or sausage, cooked through and drained
> ¼ cup chopped cooked bacon (about 4 slices)
> Frito's Scoops or your favorite corn chip, for serving

1. In a large saucepan, combine all the ingredients and cook over medium heat, stirring occasionally, until the cheese is melted and smooth. (You can also use a slow cooker, but it will take longer.)

2. Serve with Frito's Scoops or another corn chip.

RICOTTA BOARD

·MAKES 5 SERVINGS·

During a family vacation to Maine, we rented kayaks and followed a professional kayak guide up and down the coast. We think the guide might have been a little buzzed, because instead of giving us the instruction on how the kayaks worked, she just started paddling north like she was in an Olympic time trial and we were left to chase her. Despite what we were sold, there was no narration, no discussion of unique marine life, no nothing. I made a note to mention that to the owner if we could find our way back before dark.

Add to the equation the fact that the kayak my sixteen-year-old daughter, Sally, and I were in had a broken steering pedal, and we could only turn left. While everybody else was navigating easily with their feet, we had to make three left turns in order to go to the right. At one point we were two nautical miles from the rest of the group, but the leader didn't notice; she was just a dot on the horizon.

It was supposed to be fun. It was awful.

To this day I can't go on kayak.com without having a flashback.

By the way, when we got back to where we were staying, the five of us were exhausted and starving and devoured an entire meaty cheese plate that was big enough for twenty people. These days we're more interested in quality than quantity, and when it's our turn to bring out the snack bread board, this is what appears, especially on nights when we fire up the grill for a barbecue.

> 1½ cups plain whole milk Greek yogurt
> 1 cup whole milk ricotta cheese
> ½ teaspoon grated lemon zest
> Salt and freshly ground black pepper
> ⅓ cup honey
> ⅓ cup fig jelly
> 10 thick slices sourdough bread
> 2 tablespoons salted butter, at room temperature
> ½ pound sliced cured meats, such as prosciutto (rolled up with toothpicks), salami, and/or soppressata

1. Preheat a grill to high heat.
2. In a medium bowl, combine the yogurt, ricotta, lemon zest, and salt and pepper to taste and mix until smooth. Transfer the mixture to a pretty serving bowl and set aside.
3. Place the honey and fig jelly in small individual serving bowls, such as custard cups.
4. Lightly butter both sides of the sourdough slices. Grill on both sides until nicely toasted, with grill marks. Cut each slice into quarters.
5. Place the cheese bowl and the cups of honey and jelly in the middle of a large serving tray. Arrange the meats on the tray and surround with the toasted bread.

Photo on pages 22–23.

Ricotta Board
(page 21)

BAKED BUFFALO EGG ROLLS

When our daughter Mary returned home from college, we discovered that the girl who at one stage in her life would wear and eat only things that were pink (vodka sauce, cake icing, cantaloupe) had changed and would now eat only things that burned my mouth.

Eventually she settled on Buffalo sauce as her primary heat source. Buffalo Caesar salad, Buffalo deviled eggs, Buffalo oven fries—you get the idea.

There was a place nearby that made great Buffalo egg rolls, but they were fried and a little greasy, so we devised a baked version that tastes like the original when served with a creamy dressing. Mary loves these when she comes home, so we make up a batch for her, just before we take her to the Dairy Queen for a *Buffalo Blizzard*.

EGG ROLL FILLING
1 cup shredded cooked chicken breast
⅓ cup cream cheese
¼ cup crumbled blue cheese
½ cup finely shredded carrots
½ cup diced (¼-inch) celery
2 green onions, finely chopped
¼ cup Frank's RedHot Buffalo sauce

ASSEMBLY AND SERVING
12 large egg roll wrappers
Cooking spray
Store-bought blue cheese dressing or ranch dressing

1. Preheat the oven to 400°F. Line a baking sheet with parchment paper or a silicone baking mat.
2. To make the egg roll filling: In a medium bowl, mix the filling ingredients thoroughly.
3. To assemble the egg rolls: Fill a small bowl with water. Use a brush to wet the edges of a wrapper, then lay it out with a corner pointing at you. Place about 3 tablespoons of the filling just below the middle of the square. From the bottom, roll the point up and over the filling, then fold the left and right wings toward the middle, making an envelope. Tuck everything in cleanly and roll until you have a tight log. Set the egg roll aside on the prepared baking sheet and repeat to make the rest of the egg rolls.
4. Coat the egg rolls lightly but thoroughly with cooking spray and bake until golden brown, about 15 minutes.
5. Serve with the blue cheese or ranch dressing.

ROMA TOMATO FLATBREAD

On a family trip to Rome, in the shadow of the Trevi Fountain, we discovered the best pizza we had ever eaten, with a thin crust, no red sauce, and barely any cheese. Crispy, delicious, so Italian—it was perfect.

We've been making our version ever since, and whenever we bake it, it transports us back to that wonderful day, when just before we ate the pizza, we posed with a guy in gladiator getup outside the Coliseum, and after we thanked him and started walking away, he started yelling in Italian what I figure was his threat that he'd use his big plastic sword on the lot of us unless we coughed up a gratuity for the picture. We did. Then again he might have been trying to validate our parking. Don't know. We just didn't want to be *those* Americans who didn't tip a guy in a toga.

One 10.6-ounce package Wewalka
    Flatbread dough
¾ cup shredded mozzarella cheese
2 medium Roma (plum) tomatoes, each cut
    into 5 or 6 thin slices
12 orange or yellow cherry tomatoes,
    halved
1 garlic clove, minced
2 tablespoons extra-virgin olive oil
Salt and freshly ground black pepper
¼ cup jarred pepperoncini pepper rings,
    drained (optional)
Grated Parmesan cheese, for serving

1. Preheat the oven to 400°F convection (or 425°F standard).

2. Roll out the dough (Wewalka comes with parchment paper attached) on a 12 x 17-inch baking sheet. (If you use a brand without parchment paper, coat the baking sheet with oil before rolling out the dough.)

3. Sprinkle the mozzarella over the dough. This isn't a super-cheesy pie, so it's okay that not every square inch is covered. Place the Roma tomato slices in an even pattern of two rows lengthwise, then randomly scatter the cherry tomato halves on top.

4. In a small bowl, combine the garlic, olive oil, and salt and pepper to taste and whisk until smooth. Brush the mixture over the tomatoes to give them some garlic flavor. If you add the pepperoncini, don't be tempted to add more; they're just there for a little zing.

5. Bake until the edges are golden brown, 14 to 18 minutes.

6. Top with a sprinkle of grated Parmesan, then slice into pieces with a Roma tomato centered on each, and serve.

2

BREAKFAST

ONE MORNING DURING THE *FOX & FRIENDS* program, I was walking into the greenroom and saw that our new college associate was starting that day and was chatting with Karl Rove, who was an upcoming guest.

"Hi, I'm Steve Doocy. Welcome to the Dawn Patrol . . ." I said as I shook her hand.

"Hello, Mr. Doocy, I'm Daphne."

"Daphne, Karl Rove is our favorite guest because whenever we book him, he brings a dozen doughnuts, so dig in—they're delicious," I said, picking one up.

"Thank you, I'm not a big doughnut person," she said politely.

She's in college. Everybody in college is a doughnut person! I thought. Maybe she didn't want to take one and eat it in front of strangers on her first day.

"Come on, one can't kill you . . ."

"Actually, my dad . . ." she said, then stopped.

"Your dad won't let you eat a doughnut?" I inquired. It wasn't the first time I'd seen this, and I find it outrageous that helicopter parents these days have gone so overboard in parenting their children that they won't let them be kids and have a single damn doughnut.

"Trust me, your dad won't care if you have just one . . . you know, everything in moderation," I said, trying to be Mr. Helpful.

"No thanks, Mr. Doocy. Thank you, Mr. Rove."

"Okay, the box is right there if you change your mind. Eat one, because if you don't Karl will take the box back to the store and ask for a refund," I joked as I left the greenroom and went back to the studio for the next segment. She returned to her chat with Karl.

"Hey," I said to the producer listening in to my microphone from the control room.

"What?" the producer asked.

"She says her dad won't let her eat a doughnut. Who's her dad?"

There was a quiet couple seconds, and then the producer said, "You're asking who Daphne's dad is?"

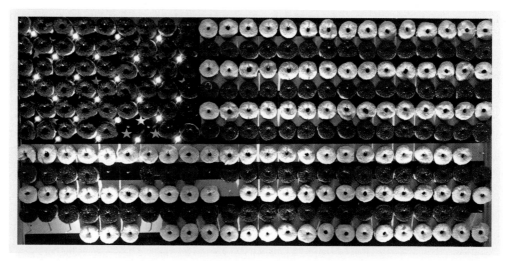

Only in America—a doughnut flag. We had to take a picture!

"Yep."

"Dr. Oz."

Okay, that was kind of a gigantic food faux pas, and I blame Karl Rove. Had he not always brought a box of doughnuts, I wouldn't have suggested to the daughter of the most famous cardiologist in the world that she should try to clog an aorta on her first day.

Daphne Oz would go on to graduate from Princeton and write a book about healthy eating habits for college kids (probably telling kids to avoid the killer foods grown-ups say are okay to eat) and then two terrific cookbooks, and she also cohosted ABC-TV's *The Chew*. And whenever I see her we have a good laugh about the "unfortunate doughnut incident of 2006."

Look, I didn't know who her family was.

Just like my future wife, Kathy. I didn't know anything about her past when we met, and as it turns out we come from completely different worlds.

I was born in Iowa and raised on a dusty limestone road in rural Kansas. Kathy grew up in a kind of glamorous neighborhood in Encino, California, where her neighbors included Judy Garland, Walt Disney, John Wayne, and directly across the street, Roy Rogers.

Kathy's dad, Joe, was a traveling salesman, and her mom, Lil, was a onetime New York model. She wasn't a big home cook; like many women in suburban Los Angeles, she hired a series of women who did all the cooking and cleaning as Lil and Kathy's grandma would watch *The Secret Storm* or some other soap opera, just killing time until the *Mike Douglas Show*.

Lil did occasionally cook hamburgers or grill chops, and her third specialty was baking a turkey in a brown paper bag from the grocery store. The bag kept the bird moist and tender, she'd explain to people who'd wonder why the bag didn't catch on fire. She never had a good explanation; she'd just say, "It just doesn't."

Turns out it was simple science. She cooked the bird at 350°F, and paper doesn't combust until 451°F. If she'd had an extra glass of Chardonnay and accidentally set the oven a bit hotter, it would have been a different story.

The bag bird *was* kind of her specialty, until one fateful Thanksgiving. Kathy's father was carefully removing it from the oven, and then from the super-hot bag, when it slipped out of his hands, leaving a foot-wide grease slick on the kitchen floor. My father-in-law lunged at the bird as it hit the linoleum, his foot skidded on the grease, and *boom*, down he went. Seeing the turkey she'd spent all day roasting on the floor, Lil approached the now-upside-down-but-still-perfect-looking bird, with an outstretched hand to retrieve it, but thanks to the combination of gravity and turkey grease, *boom*, down she went.

Disgusted by these kitchen amateurs, Kathy's seventy-five-year-old, Bronx-born grandmother went to show them both how it was done. She was able to get a single hand on a drumstick before *boom*, she, too, slipped and joined her family on the floor.

That was the last time Lil ever baked a turkey in a bag. One of the nice ladies she hired, who stayed in the room next to the den, made most of the food from that day forward.

My family was at the other end of the food chain. My dad had taken an advertising job in Kansas and was in the process of trying to make it profitable. We ate a lot of creamed peas on toast and ten-for-a-dollar pot pies. By the end of the week the only thing left in the fridge was often a pound of hamburger that my mom turned into chipped beef, which was always delicious until my dad told me that in the army they called the same thing *SOS*, which was fine until I found out what the first S stood for.

Because we had limited resources, I was taught early in life that it was a sin to let food go to waste, and whatever you had on your plate, you really needed to eat. The highlight of the week was on payday Friday, when my dad would stop at the newly opened Kentucky Fried Chicken and bring home a bucket. We had no idea what the Colonel's secret herbs and spices were, but to us it was a bucket of absolute magic.

Steve's parents, Jim and JoAnne, 1955.

My grandma Doocy didn't buy many groceries; she grew and canned her own vegetables. I remember Sundays after church when I was a little boy she'd drag me to the backyard, where we'd sneak up behind one of the two dozen penned-up chickens, and in one fluid motion she'd grab one by the leg, pick up her little hatchet, put the chicken's neck on a stump, and with surgical precision chop off the chicken's head with a single *whaaaack!*

I would watch as those headless chickens would run around the backyard for another five or ten seconds. "They don't know they're dead yet," Grandma would say. "Stephen, grab me another!"

We raised and grew our own food in part because the food selections at our local grocery were limited. I'd never had olive oil or mayonnaise until I'd gone to college, because Crisco and Miracle Whip were what you used in our house in Kansas. I know I'm making it sound like I grew up in an episode of *Little House on the Prairie*—but we did live in a little house on the actual prairie, and I did go for a while to an honest-to-goodness one-room schoolhouse.

There weren't enough kids to fill up seven different classrooms, as you would have in a typical K–6 school, so all the kids sat in the same room, which was easy because there were only eleven kids in the entire school. I was in the sixth grade with one classmate, Janine; my sister Cathy was in the third grade by herself; and my sister Lisa was in the first grade with four other kids. The school had a typical school staff—teacher, principal, nurse, janitor, and phys ed instructor—but only one person was hired for all those jobs. Mrs. Hazel Lloyd was in charge of all of us in that single room, from 8:15 a.m. until about 11:45 a.m., when she'd disappear through the north classroom door telling us to "study your lessons." At about 12:15 p.m.

that door would swing open, and there was Mrs. Lloyd, wearing an apron and hairnet so she could officially sling State of Kansas–approved starchy lunches. After lunch we were back to our lessons until 3:30 p.m., when the bus arrived and drove us all home. She was the most heroic teacher of my life, and years later when I graduated from college I wrote to her and told her how much she meant to our family. People do things like that in Kansas.

Meanwhile, growing up fifteen hundred miles away in Encino, my future wife was eating authentic quesadillas with fresh avocados grown in the same backyard where her family hosted her Sweet Sixteen party, attended by seventy-five classmates and the new neighbor kids who'd just moved there from Gary, Indiana . . . the Jackson Five. That party was legendary because some neighbor complained about the noise, and next thing she knew the guys from CHiPs (the California Highway Patrol, not Erik Estrada) flew over with a helicopter and a searchlight, then a cruiser showed up and closed them down. So Kathy had the Jackson Five and a chopper at her house in California, while meanwhile in Kansas, I was stuck in a classroom with my younger sisters, and my teacher wore a hairnet.

My point is, we grew up in very different worlds. Where I came from it seemed perfectly normal that the girl from California would know exactly how to make a delicious dinner for our first dinner date. After all, I'd grown up in a world with 4-H and home ec, and everybody could follow recipes and fend for themselves. I didn't know at the time that Kathy had spent her twenties living on take-out food, and I certainly didn't know that she'd almost burned down her apartment complex the first time she tried to cook a meal for me. I thought that smoky smell was the Gouda.

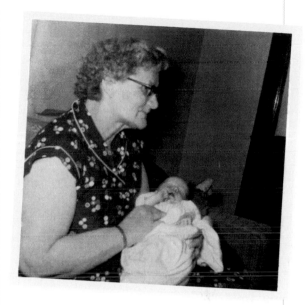

Grandma Doocy holds Steve (when not chasing chickens).

Nonetheless, her first lasagna was really terrific. At the end of that first dinner date, after hours of hearing each other's life stories and dreams for the future, I ad-libbed, "I know this is gonna scare you, but . . . someday we'll be married."

"That's nice. You should really leave now," she said. And I did.

Forty-one days later I proposed at table 52 at the legendary Washington Palm. She said yes. Six months and twenty-eight days later, we got married in the rose garden at Loose Park in Kansas City, Missouri.

For the festivities, my mother, JoAnne, had insisted on providing the cake (she had to bring something—it's what we do!), so she had the best bakery in Abilene, Kansas, prepare their top-of-the-line three-tiered lemon number filled with vanilla buttercream and decorated with festive wedding bells. My parents loaded the cake into the trunk of

There's a wedding cake melting in that trunk.

The melted cake then disappeared into a back room, and at the end of the meal, after the toasts and speeches, the cake reappeared as a single-layer lemon cake with vanilla buttercream. I thought it was delicious, but my brother-in-law said it had an "all-season radial aftertaste."

It tasted great to me, but then again I was raised on simple foods prepared simply. The only fresh fish I'd ever had was bullhead catfish pulled from the Upper Des Moines River by Grandma and me, and every other variety of seafood I'd ever eaten was either from a can or frozen from Mrs. Paul's. That could be why our first fight as a married couple was about fish, a topic on which I was clueless.

the Doocy family K-car and drove 155 miles across Kansas, directly to the park, on what was observed by more than a few attendees as the "hottest damn day" of the year. They proceeded to park the car in direct sun and watched us get married for about an hour. My dad knew something was up when we returned to his car for the short drive to the reception and he noticed yellow frosting dripping out by the muffler.

"Mom promised wedding cake, but she brought wedding soup!" I joked in the voice of someone who'd just had two glasses of warm Champagne while standing in a fountain to cool off. I was doing my best to minimize my mom's broken heart over a melted wedding cake.

After a short trip to the reception restaurant, my father took the leaning tower of buttercream to our waiter and asked him what they could do.

"How about I give everybody a straw?" he joked. Nobody laughed.

Our wedding day, 1986.

We went to Hawaii on our honeymoon and stayed at a place we really couldn't afford (we paid in points). The first night the waiter presented us with the dinner specials, then asked if we had questions. Trying to act like a fish aficionado, I asked nonchalantly, "What's your mahi-mahi this evening?"

"The mahi-mahi is the mahi-mahi," he said, looking at me as if he was trying to gauge my blood alcohol level. I was sober, but I told him I'd just recently been educated by a waiter in Kansas that mahi-mahi is a generic restaurant term, like "soup du jour."

"Mahi-mahi," I informed him, apparently for the first time, "means 'fish of the day.'"

Probably hoping not to lose his 15 percent tip, the waiter said he was a marine biologist who'd moved to Hawaii to study marine life, and mahi-mahi was an actual species of fish. He pointed to a big chart on the wall and said, "We refer to our fish of the day as 'fish du jour.'"

Humiliated by the fish guy, I was suddenly in a bad mood, but no worse than my wife, who was wondering what kind of country bumpkin she'd just married. She stopped talking to me for three days, which is rough on your honeymoon.

By the end of the trip, we were laughing about it, but to this day when we're in a restaurant and that fish species is written on a chalkboard or a menu, Kathy will point and mouth the word "mahi-mahi," with that *How the Grinch Stole Christmas* grin.

I guess the lesson of our early days is that it is possible for two people from different worlds to find each other and fall in love over a nice meal and some good conversation. The key is finding some *common ground* in the kitchen.

As long as that *common ground* is not covered in turkey grease . . .

Boom!

EGG IN A NEST

Thirty years ago we started making the classic egg in a nest from *Disney's Family Cookbook*. It was simply an egg fried in a hole cut in a piece of bread.

"Dad, why do they call it egg in a nest? It's egg in toast," Mary, our future lawyer, said.

She was right, so Mary inspired me to devise a version of egg in a nest that looks exactly like an egg in a nest. After twenty years of trying, I hit pay dirt when I realized that hash browns arranged in a circle look like a bird's nest!

Eureka!

If there were a lifetime achievement award for innovation in breakfast foods that look like their names, I would hope Mary would nominate me and not the guy who invented the Pop-Tart.

Cooking spray
4 cups frozen hash browns, thawed to room
    temperature
Salt and freshly ground black pepper
4 large eggs
¼ cup shredded Cheddar cheese
1 green onion, thinly sliced, for garnish
Ketchup, Frank's RedHot sauce, or sriracha,
    for serving

1. Preheat the oven to 350°F. Coat a baking sheet with cooking spray.

2. Place 4 equal mounds of the hash browns on the prepared baking sheet. To make each nest, use your fingers to form a classic round nest shape, leaving about 1 inch of empty space in the center, where the egg will go. Use the back of a spatula or measuring cup to press down on the potatoes, fusing them together. Coat the nests liberally with cooking spray (this will make them fused and crispy), then lightly salt and pepper them to taste.

3. Bake until the nests are mostly golden around the edges, about 20 minutes.

4. Reshape the nests as needed, spooning any loose hash browns into the nests. Crack an egg into the middle of each nest, sprinkle with salt and pepper, and bake for about 15 minutes more for no runny yolks.

5. Sprinkle about a tablespoon of shredded Cheddar on top, followed by some green onions if you like. Remove the nests to plates using a spatula and serve as is or with a squirt of ketchup, Frank's RedHot sauce, or sriracha.

STEVE'S 3 A.M. BREAKFAST SMOOTHIE

Never not once have I ever hit the snooze button on my alarm clock when it goes off at 3:27 a.m. to wake me up for *Fox & Friends*. I'm getting up with not one extra minute to spare.

For breakfast for the last ten years, I've had a bowl of steel-cut oatmeal with raisins and almond milk, plus this smoothie. During the summer months, I swap in fresh fruits for the frozen. But the biggest drawback is that I make this in the blender, when everybody is asleep . . . and it's noisy.

By now my wife (and the kids, if they're home) is used to hearing that noise in the three o'clock hour, but it's also a subtle way for me to remind the family that while they are snug in their beds, waiting to get up three hours later, Dad is on his way to work, driving twenty-five miles through the dark of night to provide for his family, because that's what responsible dads do.

Note to snoozing Mrs. Doocy: That blender had better be washed by the time I get home for lunch . . . just saying.

3 large frozen strawberries
½ cup frozen blueberries
½ scoop vanilla whey protein powder
½ tablespoon ground flaxseed
½ cup fresh orange juice
¼ cup unsweetened almond milk, plus more as needed
1 banana, cut into 3 or 4 pieces
Whipped cream, a few banana slices, a strawberry, or 3 blueberries on a decorative toothpick, for garnish

1. This is a simple recipe, but I tell you—the order you put the items in the blender makes a difference when it comes to efficient mixing and easy cleanup. Place all the ingredients in the blender in the order listed above. Blend until smooth, 45 seconds to 1 minute. The protein powder makes it really thick, so add a little more almond milk to thin it down if you like.

2. If you're not in a hurry to get to work, you can be festive and garnish with whipped cream or fresh fruit.

3. Drink it immediately. If the blender has awoken the whole house, invite them for a sip.

SALLY'S GRAB 'N' GO BUS BREAKFAST

Please do not call the authorities, but many a morning after a holiday, when it was time to feed the kids breakfast, Kathy would serve them a piece of leftover pie . . . with whipped cream . . . or a scoop of ice cream. We are not big on bagels, so if there was a pie in the house at 7 a.m., it was probably gone by 8 a.m., and the kids went to school with a sugar high. It's not against the law . . . in our town. We checked.

Now our kids are all healthy eaters, and Sally patterned this recipe after something she had for breakfast in New York. We make up a batch of these egg muffin cups, then on the way out the door Sally pops one in the microwave and she's on her way to work, where she'll design an innovative advertising plan or do important shopping at JCrew.com.

Cooking spray
¼ red bell pepper, thinly sliced
Garlic powder
Salt and freshly ground black pepper
¾ cup liquid egg whites (or the whites from 6 large eggs)
¼ cup fat-free half-and-half
4 tablespoons grated Cheddar cheese
Sriracha or Tabasco sauce, for serving (optional)

4 cupcake baking cups (if you're taking these to go)

1. Preheat the oven to 350°F. Coat 4 cups of a muffin tin with cooking spray.

2. Place the bell pepper slices on a microwave-safe plate and add a dash each of garlic powder, salt, and black pepper. Cover with plastic wrap and microwave 60 to 90 seconds, until tender-crisp.

3. In a 1-cup measuring cup with a pour spout, combine the egg whites and half-and-half. Add a little salt and black pepper to your taste and then whisk until smooth. Add 2 tablespoons of the Cheddar and give it a good mix.

4. Pour ¼ cup of the egg mixture into each of the muffin cups, then divide the bell pepper among them. Bake for 10 minutes, then sprinkle ½ tablespoon of the remaining Cheddar onto each. Bake until the eggs reach the desired firmness, 6 to 8 minutes.

5. Let the egg bites rest at room temperature for a few minutes before spooning them out. If you're going to grab and go, place each egg bite into a cupcake baking cup for portability. Otherwise, grab a fork and enjoy. A squirt of sriracha or Tabasco can add a little zing if you need a jump start in the morning.

NOTE: *These keep well in the fridge, and 35 to 45 seconds in the microwave will reheat them to the perfect temperature. Just let them rest a bit and eat when cooled to your liking.*

EGGS McDOOCY

When the kids were little, Sunday mornings after church they would beg for us to stop on the way home at McDonald's for the holy grail of breakfast foods, the Egg McMuffin. As they got older, it was harder to get them to church, but they still had to eat, so we started making our own version of the EMcM.

You could use English muffins, as McDonald's does, but we bake up a fresh puff pastry version that makes it look like Dad drove to the McDonald's on the Champs-Élysées . . . which would be hard because there's an ocean between our house and that McDonald's. So until Elon Musk invents the AquaCar, we'll be baking these up on Sunday mornings stateside.

Cooking spray
6 large eggs, plus 1 for the egg wash
Salt and freshly ground black pepper
One 13.2-ounce package Wewalka Puff
   Pastry dough
6 slices thick-cut Canadian bacon
½ cup shredded Cheddar cheese

1. Preheat the oven to 350°F convection (or 375°F standard). Line a baking sheet with parchment paper.
2. Coat a 3- or 4-inch-wide mug or ramekin with cooking spray. Crack an egg into it. Gently break the yolk with a fork, stabbing 3 or 4 times so it

doesn't go nuclear during cooking. Add salt and pepper to taste, then cover it loosely in plastic wrap and microwave for about 45 seconds to a minute until it's starting to firm up. Spoon the egg out of its container; set aside. Repeat until you've got six half-cooked eggs.
3. Roll out the puff pastry and use a 3½-inch biscuit cutter to cut out 12 rounds.
4. Place 6 of the rounds on the lined baking sheet, spaced a few inches apart. Place a slice of Canadian bacon on each and sprinkle a little Cheddar on top.
5. Place one of the eggs atop each bacon/cheese pile. More Cheddar on top of that, and try to flatten each mound so that it's level (if it's not, once the pastry puffs up, your sandwich will lean to one side). Repeat this process until you've got six of them assembled.
6. Finally, place the remaining six pastry rounds on the tops on the sandwiches.
7. Whisk the egg for the egg wash and add in a splash of water. Paint some egg wash on the top of each pastry round and bake until the crust is golden and the cheese is melted, about 20 minutes.
8. Remove the McDoocys, let them rest only a few minutes, and serve.

BREAKFAST PIZZA

•MAKES 4 SERVINGS•

Kathy made the kids' lunches almost every day of their school lives. Inside the brown bags she would always leave them a little surprise, such as a piece of candy, a funny card, or a little note about how much she loved them. In return the kids would bring their lunch bags back at the end of the day, mostly empty, but always appreciative of her effort.

One morning when Peter was in the second grade, his teacher, Mrs. Ralph, called and said, "I know you made Peter's lunch . . . but today is pizza day. He wants a piece, but he doesn't want to hurt your feelings."

Of course Kathy gave the green light for Peter to have pizza, and just to make sure she never missed it again, as soon as the school lunch calendar would come out, she'd write PIZZA in big letters on the month-at-a-glance calendar that hung in our kitchen.

But here's the part they don't tell you about pizza day at school. Some days the pizza was great and other days it was so greasy that the kids would have to lie down on the playground during recess to recover. Some moms we know had to go to school and cart their kids home. And what would those kids do when the next pizza day rolled around? Order more. Come on, it's pizza day.

This recipe is our diabolical way to be the best parents in the world: We make our kids pizza for breakfast.

1 tablespoon extra-virgin olive oil
5 large eggs
¼ cup fat-free half-and-half
Salt and freshly ground black pepper
4 slices bacon (turkey bacon works great, too)
One 15-ounce ball prepared pizza dough
1 cup shredded Cheddar cheese
½ tomato, seeded and diced
1 or 2 green onions, finely chopped

1. Preheat the oven to 400°F. Lightly grease a pizza pan or baking sheet with the olive oil.
2. In a small bowl, whisk the eggs with the half-and-half and salt and pepper to taste
3. In a medium skillet scramble the eggs over medium heat until done to your liking, with pieces as small and uniform as possible. Set aside.
4. Microwave the bacon for 3 to 5 minutes, depending on your microwave, until browned and crispy. Cut into small pieces and set aside.
5. Roll out the dough to fit a 16-inch pizza pan or baking sheet and lay it in the pan.
6. Evenly sprinkle the crust with the scrambled eggs, Cheddar, bacon bits, tomato, and green onions.
7. Bake until the crust is golden and crispy and the cheese is melted, 12 to 15 minutes. Slice into four pieces and serve. *Mamma mia*, that's an easy breakfast!

BRUNCH BUNDT

• MAKES 10 TO 12 SERVINGS •

In our family, we all generally like the same foods, although I really don't enjoy hibachi places where they cook on the table and throw shrimp in your mouth like a seal. So Kathy takes the kids to those places when I'm out of town. Or she did—until the time she got a chef who used the same utensils on the chicken, steak, and lobster from start to finish. "Hey, you need a new spatula . . . ," she said after half an hour with no utensil change, worrying about the potential for cross contamination or salmonella. "Hey, buddy, I'm from the New York State Health Department and that's not sanitary. I'm ready to close this place down." There could have been a language problem, because he kept chopping until he made a flaming volcano out of a yellow onion. She took the kids home and never went back.

This recipe has everything we like to eat for breakfast—ham, eggs, Tater Tots, and freshly baked biscuits, all made in a Bundt pan. Sally, our kid in New York ad sales, calls it "Everything BUNDT the kitchen sink." Finally some truth in advertising.

BUNDT
1 tablespoon butter
8 large eggs
½ cup fat-free half-and-half or milk
½ teaspoon salt
¼ teaspoon freshly ground black pepper
1 cup grated Cheddar cheese
1 cup frozen Tater Tots
2 cups cubed cooked ham
1 can Pillsbury Grands Flaky Layers Original Biscuits

CHEESE SAUCE
1 tablespoon butter
1½ tablespoons flour
⅛ teaspoon salt
1 cup milk
½ cup grated Cheddar cheese

1. To make the Bundt: Preheat the oven to 400°F. Coat a Bundt pan with the butter.

2. In a large bowl, combine the eggs, half-and-half, salt, and pepper and whisk until very smooth. Mix in the Cheddar, then the Tater Tots and ham.

3. Open the can of biscuits and cut each one into at least 6 pieces. Separate them and put them in the egg batter individually, mixing as you go to coat the dough on all sides. Give one good final stir.

4. Pour the biscuit and egg mixture evenly into the Bundt pan. Bake until golden brown on top, 45 to 50 minutes.

5. About 10 minutes before it's done, make the sauce: In a small saucepan, melt the butter over medium heat. Whisk in the flour and salt, stirring and cooking for about 2 minutes. Slowly pour in the milk and whisk until the lumps are gone. Keep stirring until it gets thicker and bubbles, 3 to 5 minutes, then stir in the Cheddar just until melted and smooth. Cover and set aside, keeping the sauce warm.

6. Use a butter knife or small spatula to loosen the bread from the pan, then place a plate over the pan and carefully invert it so that the brunch Bundt sits regally on the plate.

7. Lightly drizzle the cheese sauce over the bread, or serve it on the side. Place the rest in a small serving pitcher for people who want more cheese.

BAKED EGGS BENNY

Our favorite fancy hotel breakfast when we're traveling is eggs Benedict, but the sauce and perfect egg poaching can be daunting, so at home we use these puff pastry shells, which make them look like they rolled off the line at the Cordon Bleu. You can make your own hollandaise sauce, but the packet stuff is so simple and fast.

These look so fancy that if you're serving this for brunch guests they'll assume you bought them premade, so save the puff pastry box to prove you made them from *almost* scratch.

> One 10-ounce package Pepperidge Farm
>   Puff Pastry Shells, thawed
> 6 large eggs
> Salt and freshly ground black pepper
> 1 envelope Knorr Hollandaise Sauce Mix
> 1 cup milk
> 4 tablespoons (½ stick) butter
> Hot sauce (optional)
> 6 pieces breakfast ham or Canadian bacon
> Chopped chives, hot sauce, or paprika, for
>   garnish

1. Preheat the oven to 425°F.

2. Bake the puff pastry shells according to the package directions. Just know they start out flat and blow up just like the picture on the box. Make sure you place the dough rounds with the tops facing up (that's the side with the deeply scored circle).

3. When they're golden and beautiful, remove them from the oven (but keep the oven on). Using a fork, remove the pastry tops and dig out any extra pastry to make a clean pastry ring. Crack 1 egg into each shell and salt and pepper lightly.

4. Bake for 16 to 18 minutes, then give the pastry shells a jiggle to check whether the eggs are as soft or firm as you like.

5. Meanwhile, prepare the hollandaise sauce according to the envelope directions, using the milk and butter. Add a squirt of hot sauce if you like (we do). Set aside and keep warm.

6. In a microwave, heat the ham or Canadian bacon just until warm (no more than 30 seconds).

7. When the eggs are done, place a piece of ham or bacon on each plate, lay a baked egg pastry on top, and drizzle with as much of the hollandaise sauce as you like. Garnish with a sprinkle of chives, a squirt of hot sauce, or a dash of paprika. Serve immediately.

3

SOUPS AND SALADS

DURING OUR SALAD DAYS AS A newlywed couple, Kathy made the same thing every night for dinner . . . reservations.

I know that's an old joke, but she didn't know how to cook, and she didn't need to know, because when she lived in New York as a single woman, she lived in a building with a diner downstairs and ordered takeout for every single meal. Even breakfast, which was usually just toast.

"Wait . . . you didn't know how to make toast?"

"I didn't have a toaster!" she insisted, which didn't actually answer my question.

When we were first married and living in Washington, DC, Kathy could make lasagna but not much else, so we ate out a lot, mainly for survival. When our son, Peter, was born and his baptism party rolled around, Kathy invited our friends over, then went to a legendary fancy food store called Larimer's and bought a ham and cake. Hoping to impress in her role as new mom, she wanted the food to look homemade. It did not—it was too perfect. It was so perfect that our New York guests told us to take pictures of it. To this day we have a dozen pictures of the ham from various angles, and one of the kid who was baptized.

When we moved to the DC suburbs, there weren't as many good restaurants nearby and Kathy vowed to learn how to cook. She went to the Barnes & Noble in Tysons Corner, Virginia, and bought *one* cookbook. She didn't know anything about the author or the recipes; she just liked the picture on the cover. It looked delicious!

In the coming months, after many agonizing attempts at cooking, we discovered that she had

Sally dove into chowder after every meet.

bought one of the most complicated cookbooks ever printed in English. The recipes in the book called for unheard-of kitchen tools (where does one buy a *cloche*?), used unexplained cooking techniques (". . . your bain-marie will control the custard temperature . . ."), and required ingredients (acerola, boletes, hyssop) not sold in our zip code.

So Kathy started asking friends and neighbors for some easier recipes and tips on cooking. Most were happy to share; our friend Maureen showed her how to make a roasted chicken: salt, pepper, a squirt of lemon juice, and baked first at 425°F, then down to 350°F until the pop-up timer popped up. *Lesson learned: Simple can be delicious.* We made Frank Perdue richer with that chicken, which we've roasted once a week for thirty years.

When Kathy asked her friend Julie for the recipe to her addictive salad dressing, Julie replied, "It's just the recipe on the box." So Kathy brought home Good Seasons Italian Salad Dressing and tried it half a dozen times, but it never tasted as good as Julie's. So the next time we went over we watched her make it, and it turned out rather than use the called-for ⅔ cup of olive oil, she used 1 full cup of *bacon grease*, from the pound of bacon that was crumbled on top of everything. *Lesson learned: It's okay to upgrade ingredients to make things taste better.* Also, invest heavily in Lipitor stock.

We'd had a wonderful meal at another friend's house, and Kathy politely asked the baker if she'd share her chocolate cake recipe. "I'd love to, Kath!" The friend carefully wrote it on an index card, re-checked the ingredients, and sent us on our way. Kathy spent an hour re-creating it the next Sunday and it turned out . . . awful. She tried again, and the second attempt was even worse. Kathy asked a different friend who was an expert baker to look at the recipe and tell her what she was doing wrong. After a ten-second glance at the card, she announced, "There's no sugar."

Hmmmm . . . the single most important ingredient had been left out. Could it have been sabotage? *Lesson learned: Some people don't want to share their secrets . . . and that's okay.*

By the way, the neighbor who shared this recipe was the same woman whose mother had grown so weary of her cranky husband that she wanted to ask for a divorce, but their Virginia country club did not allow divorcees as members. After the husband's second heart attack he was put on a restrictive diet of no red meat, low salt, and absolutely *no butter,* which garnered nightly dinner reviews like "This tastes like crap!"

Getting tired of hearing lousy reviews, his wife apparently picked up some new recipes, because the food suddenly tasted terrific. He was asking for

seconds again, and thirds. But after a few months he was gaining weight, his blood pressure was soaring, and he was wheezing by the end of his morning walks. His cardiologist was mystified, and so was he until he walked into the kitchen after a nap to discover his wife was melting a stick of butter in the cauliflower mashed potatoes, with a side of salad dressing that was 75 percent liquefied butter (apparently she didn't have Julie's bacon grease Italian dressing recipe, which would have achieved the same results).

"Are you trying to kill me?" he asked. She just kept stirring.

"Maybe we should go out to eat," he said, and they did, and they still do, for every meal. As of this writing, they're still married and go to that country club twice a week. She doesn't cook, so she's on easy street, and he's on South Beach—the diet, that is.

Ever expanding her repertoire of recipes via those slim booklets you find next to the grocery store cashier, Kathy was also gathering cookbooks with easier recipes. An early favorite was *The Silver Palate Good Times Cookbook.* One summer day I asked her to try to make potato salad. She found a recipe in *Silver Palate* and followed every instruction until she could announce proudly that it was perfect!

She asked me to carry the very heavy bowl of potato salad to the table, which I did as she finished prepping dinner in the kitchen. She brought in the London broil and started to sit down, then began screaming, "What happened to my potato salad???"

Actually, nothing *happened* to it. However, as a state fair blue-ribbon-winning chef myself, I felt that it lacked something, so I added what my mom always put on the top of her potato salad: paprika and plenty of it, just like every cook in Kansas. Clearly the *Silver Palate* authors had left it out of the recipe, so I added it as a public service.

Kathy was furious.

In hindsight, Mom had always made a traditional potato salad, which consisted of white potatoes, white onions, white eggs, and snow-white Miracle Whip. It begged for some color, so she'd add the red badge of paprika. Kathy's potato salad was like a color wheel explosion, with green, orange, red, and white. It didn't need anything on top—especially a random red.

"It . . . was . . . perfect . . ." she said, her voice trailing off. I knew I'd hurt her feelings; she was angry that she'd spent two hours making something that her husband vandalized—in four shakes from a spice jar.

And with that, *mahi-mahi* had company, and it was *paprika*.

Lesson learned: Never screw with somebody's potato salad, or anything else they've invested time and energy into creating. We all have our own ideas of what should be in a recipe, but if you want to go rogue and doctor somebody else's masterpiece, ask first—or just make it yourself.

After my little paprika experiment I was worried that Kathy was still angry, and I'd come home to discover she'd gotten a new recipe from that movie—you know, the one in which that nice lady Glenn Close shows how to cook a rabbit.

That's where I wake up in the dream, every time.

There's something about wives with knives.

But I will say that I'm sure if Kathy served rabbit, it would be delicious . . . if properly prepared with just a dash of . . . never mind.

PETER'S PEANUT SOUP

·MAKES 10 TO 12 SERVINGS·

When the kids were little we lived in Virginia, and one summer we took a family road trip to Colonial Williamsburg. (If you've never been, go—it's great.) We bought three-corner colonial hats, watched the parade, and took a carriage ride; and I remember our grade school–age Peter Doocy turning colonial comic and asking us, "What's Thomas Jefferson's favorite dessert?"

We didn't know.

"Monti-Jell-O," he said, cackling. And who says public schools don't work?

On the King's Arms Tavern menu we spotted cream of peanut soup. It was described as a Southern favorite garnished with peanuts and served with sippets. I ordered it to find out what a sippet was. This was years before Google, but I'll help you out: A sippet is a small piece of toast for your soup. The sippet was okay, but the soup was a *wow*, and it became a family favorite. When Kathy took Peter on a college tour of Virginia universities, every time he saw this on a menu, he'd order a bowl. Years later when he was covering the National Governor's Conference in Williamsburg, he ate this with every meal. Except breakfast. It's that good.

Thanks to the King's Arms Tavern at Colonial Williamsburg for sharing their famous recipe.

4 tablespoons (½ stick) unsalted butter
1 medium onion, finely chopped
2 celery stalks, finely chopped
3 tablespoons flour
8 cups (2 quarts) chicken stock or low-sodium canned chicken stock
2 cups creamy peanut butter
1¾ cups light cream or half-and-half
Finely chopped salted peanuts, for garnish

1. In a large saucepan or soup pot, melt the butter over medium heat. Add the onion and celery and cook, stirring often, until softened, 3 to 5 minutes.

2. Stir in the flour and cook 2 minutes longer.

3. Pour in the chicken stock, increase the heat to high, and bring to a boil, stirring constantly. Reduce the heat to medium and cook, stirring often, until slightly reduced and thickened, about 15 minutes. Strain through a sieve set over a large bowl, pushing hard on the solids to extract as much flavor as possible. Return the liquid to the saucepan or pot.

4. Whisk the peanut butter and cream into the liquid. Warm over low heat, whisking often, for about 5 minutes. Do not boil.

5. Serve warm, garnished with the chopped peanuts.

FIRE-ROASTED TOMATO SOUP AND GRILLED CHEESE CROUTONS

There were two times growing up when we ate a lot of grilled cheese sandwiches and tomato soup: Lent (for obvious reasons) and downpours. My mom used to say, "Stephen, rainy days are for naps," which was code for "Stephen, I'm stuck in the house with you, you're hopped up on sugar cookies and Kool-Aid, and you need to pipe down!" I'm sure she meant it in the nicest way, but now as a parent, I know when you're stuck in the house with a bunch of kids, a sleeping child is a beautiful thing.

Back then Mom just warmed up a can of Campbell's, but Kathy started making our own tomato soup from scratch. Our friend Chris had the idea of cutting up tiny grilled cheese sandwich croutons that float on the top of the soup. Because they're not full-size sandwiches, they're just a tasty bite that makes this evolution in the science of grilled cheese clever and delicious.

GRILLED CHEESE CROUTONS
Butter
4 slices white bread
2 slices American cheese

SOUP
2 tablespoons extra-virgin olive oil
1 medium onion, cut into medium dice
3 garlic cloves, minced
Two 14-ounce cans diced fire-roasted tomatoes (and their juice)
2 cups vegetable stock
2 tablespoons minced fresh basil
⅛ teaspoon red pepper flakes
½ cup heavy cream
¼ cup grated Parmesan cheese

1. To make the grilled cheese croutons: Butter 2 pieces of the bread on one side. Place a single piece of cheese between the pieces with the butter side facing out. Repeat to make a second sandwich.

2. In a large skillet, toast the sandwiches on both sides over medium heat until golden and a little melty inside, 2 to 4 minutes. Cut off and discard the crusts, then cut the sandwiches into 1-inch squares. Set aside.

3. To make the soup: In a medium saucepan, warm the olive oil, onion, and garlic over medium-high heat and sauté until the onion is almost translucent, 2 to 3 minutes. Add the tomatoes, stock, and basil and simmer about 10 minutes, until thoroughly heated.

4. Using an immersion blender in the saucepan, puree the soup until just slightly grainy. (Alternatively, puree the soup in a blender, working in batches and taking care not to fill the blender too full of hot liquid. Return the soup to the saucepan.)

5. Reduce the heat under the soup to medium and add the pepper flakes, cream, and Parmesan. Simmer for 5 minutes (do not bring to a boil).

6. To serve, ladle the soup into bowls and float as many of the grilled cheese croutons on top as you'd like. Three or four are a nice start. Place the rest in a serving bowl for when somebody asks for another . . . and they will.

BACON-CORN CHOWDER

Growing up in Kansas and Iowa, one of the best-paying jobs for kids my age was also the worst job imaginable: detasseling corn. You reach up to the top of a six-foot-tall corn plant and pull off the top "tassel" part of the corn and drop it on the ground. This was the kind of manual labor young men did on the hottest days of the summer, so they would concentrate on personal responsibility and integrity rather than hang out at the billiards saloon, chewing tobacco and flirting with pool hall girls.

I hated the job so much that it left a bad taste in my mouth, figuratively and literally. I couldn't stand to eat or even smell sweet corn for about twenty years after that. But that's far in my rearview mirror, and now when summer rolls around, we serve corn at almost every meal.

6 to 8 slices bacon, cut into 1-inch pieces
1 small Vidalia (sweet) onion, cut into medium dice
2 garlic cloves, minced
3 tablespoons flour
2 cups chicken stock
2 cups milk, warmed in a microwave for 90 seconds, until hot but not boiling
1 pound baby red potatoes, unpeeled, cut into ½-inch cubes
One 4-ounce can chopped green chilies, drained
2 teaspoons herbes de Provence
Salt and freshly ground black pepper
6 ears corn, kernels cut from the cobs
1 cup grated Cheddar cheese
Crusty bread or crostini, for serving

1. In a large soup pot or Dutch oven, fry the bacon over medium-high heat until crispy brown. Set aside and drain most of the grease from the pot. Add the onion and sauté until soft and golden, 4 to 5 minutes. Add the garlic and stir for 1 minute. Sprinkle on the flour, add the stock, and give a stir. Stir in the milk, potatoes, chilies, herbes de Provence, 1 teaspoon salt, and ¼ teaspoon pepper and bring the soup to a boil. Reduce the heat to a simmer and cook for 20 minutes.

2. Add the corn and simmer 20 minutes more, making sure the potatoes are nice and done. Taste and adjust to your liking with more salt or pepper.

3. Remove from the heat, stir in the Cheddar and bacon, and serve with a side of crusty bread or crostini.

SWIM TEAM POTATO CHOWDER

•MAKES 4 SERVINGS•

All of our kids played team sports in high school, but the hardest sport of all was the one Sally picked as her specialty . . . swimming. Not the fastest athlete on a team of standouts, she used a clever strategy to make the team. She specialized in the one event nobody wanted to do: the 500-meter race. Twenty laps, the longest race. It was torture.

At every meet she swam with all her heart, and by her senior year she was the varsity team captain. That's the good news. The bad news was that practices would run until 11 p.m. on a school night, and she'd be starving by the time she left the YMCA. So Kathy would have a batch of this soup waiting almost every winter night and Sally would eat it in the kitchen with her wet hair wrapped in a towel and smelling like she was working nights at the Clorox bleach factory. The glamour of varsity sports.

3 large Yukon Gold potatoes, peeled and quartered
3 cups milk
Salt and freshly ground black pepper
1 tablespoon butter
4 ounces cream cheese, at room temperature
½ cup grated Cheddar cheese
4 green onions, chopped
Crusty bread or crostini, for serving

1. Place the potatoes in a large soup pot and add water to cover. Bring to a boil over medium-high heat and cook until the potatoes are very tender, about 15 minutes.

2. Drain the potatoes, return them to the pot, and quickly add the milk. Season with salt and pepper. Give a good mash with a potato masher, leaving no big chunks. Bring to a simmer over medium-high heat and stir until the mixture thickens, about 2 minutes. Reduce the heat to low, add the butter and cream cheese, and whisk until smooth.

3. Stir in the Cheddar and green onions. Serve with a side of crusty bread or crostini.

SEA ISLAND BRUNSWICK STEW

•MAKES 4 QUARTS (AND FREEZES WELL!)•

From the first time our family went to Sea Island on the Georgia coast, we realized it was a magical place. Every vacation we'd spend at least one night (before bingo) having the sunset dinner on Rainbow Island, where there was always a giant pot of Brunswick stew waiting. It almost always filled us up with no room for the rest of their big buffet—but somehow we managed.

It's the heartiest stew in the world, and we just love it. Years ago, Kathy asked one of our friends who lived on Sea Island for their recipe, which we enjoyed for the longest time, but for this cookbook we got an *official* Sea Island Resort version of the stew, and it's *great* . . . just know we have adapted it.

Sea Island Resort spends a day to smoke their own pork butt, but on weekends when we make this, Mrs. Doocy always has a honey-do list waiting for me, so we buy already smoked pork butt from our local BBQ joint to save time.

It's a warm treat on a chilly night, and just one bite takes us back to Sea Island, which to this day is one of our favorite vacation spots in America.

1 to 2 tablespoons extra-virgin olive oil
2 cups diced (½-inch) onions
2 pounds smoked and cooked pork butt (from your local BBQ joint or fresh leftovers)
6 cups ham stock (we use Better Than Bouillon brand ham base)
One 28-ounce can diced tomatoes
One 6-ounce can tomato paste
2 medium potatoes, unpeeled, cut into ½-inch cubes
One 14-ounce box frozen corn kernels, thawed
One 16-ounce bag frozen lima beans, thawed
One 13-ounce bag frozen peas, thawed
2 teaspoons hot sauce, such as Frank's RedHot, plus more as needed
1 cup barbecue sauce, plus more as needed
Salt and freshly ground black pepper
1 tablespoon liquid smoke, to taste

1. In a large soup pot, heat the olive oil over medium-high heat. Add the onions and sweat until translucent, 5 to 8 minutes. If your already cooked pork butt is not shredded, take two forks and shred into pieces. The smaller the strands, the better. Remove any extra fat. Once done add the smoked pork to the pot and then the ham stock and bring to a simmer. Stir in the diced tomatoes and tomato paste and simmer for about 45 minutes over medium-low heat.

2. Add the potatoes and cook until tender, 15 to 20 minutes. When the potatoes are almost done, add the corn, lima beans, and peas and cook until tender, 5 to 7 minutes.

3. Finish with the hot sauce and barbecue sauce to your personal taste (add more as desired). Simmer the stew for 5 minutes, season with salt, pepper, and a little liquid smoke to taste, and serve.

SALLY'S SIDE SALAD

Our sweet youngest child, Sally, has become our designated dining-out expert and takes over the early ordering when we go out to eat. As soon as she sits down, she scans the menu and orders appetizers for the table. She's developed a sophisticated palate, on par with that of a *New York Times* restaurant critic. In fact, she once posted a two-star review on OpenTable and the restaurant called to apologize and begged her to come back.

She did not. *Burn . . .*

She's changed from a kid who wanted to eat only Murry's French Toast Sticks for breakfast and chicken fingers for all other meals. Her Instant Messenger nickname was chickenfingers4ever.

Now she knows and appreciates great food and is not shy about her meal requests at home. This is the salad she ad-libbed on the phone one summer afternoon, when she was dictating exactly what she wanted us to make for dinner, as if she was calling Takeout Taxi.

I've got to admit, it's delicious and goes with almost anything. Okay, maybe not Murry's French Toast Sticks . . . but you get the idea.

2 ears corn, unhusked (if out of season, use 1 cup frozen corn kernels, cooked)
Half an 8-ounce ball fresh mozzarella cheese, cut into 4 pieces
1 avocado, pitted, peeled, and cut into ½-inch cubes
1 beefsteak tomato, cut into ½-inch cubes
3 tablespoons store-bought pesto (we use Costco's Kirkland brand)
Salt and freshly ground black pepper
2 green onions, green tops only, sliced
Balsamic glaze, for drizzling

1. Pull back the corn husks but keep them intact. Remove the silk and put the husks back in place. Microwave the corn on high for 6 minutes, then set aside to cool.

2. In a medium bowl, combine the mozzarella, avocado, and tomato. Peel back the corn husks and carefully cut the corn directly into the bowl. Top with the pesto. Add salt and pepper to taste and stir to combine. Garnish with the green onions.

3. Plate the salads, add balsamic glaze in a festive zigzag drizzle, and serve.

Photo on page 163.

BURRATA, TOMATO, AND PESTO SALAD

Earlier in this cookbook, we recounted the greatest meal of our lives, when we were the guests of Daniel Boulud, then running the show at New York's legendary Le Cirque. Today Mr. Boulud has a number of restaurants across America, and most of the food is too perfect to even attempt to re-create at home. But at his Café Boulud in Palm Beach we order his burrata and tomato salad whenever it pops up on the menu, and it's one that regular people can tackle at home.

This is our own interpretation, with some summertime extras added to his concept; and if he ever came to dinner at our place, we think he'd like it. Then again, if he came to dinner, we'd insist that *he* do the cooking, so we'd wind up with his version, not ours.

4 medium heirloom tomatoes (in a variety
    of colors if possible)
1 cup store-bought pesto (we like Costco's
    Kirkland brand)

Four 2-ounce burrata balls (4-ounce balls
    will also work)
Freshly ground black pepper
Basil, for beauty

1. Core the tomatoes, cut each into 5 or 6 wedges, and place them in a medium bowl. Add 2 tablespoons of the pesto, give a stir, and set aside.

2. Place a burrata ball in the middle of each of four salad plates, then circle it with a swirl of 2 or 3 tablespoons pesto. Dividing evenly, surround the burrata balls with tomatoes.

3. Drizzle a little more pesto on the burrata balls, give them a grind of pepper, and festoon with some thinly shredded basil.

4. *[dream sequence] "Délicieux, Doocys!" Mr. Boulud says after dinner at our house. Then he does the dishes and sharpens our knives.*

Photo on pages 62–63.

Burrata, Tomato, and
Pesto Salad (page 61)

KATHY'S CALIFORNIA COBB

Growing up just over the hill from the legendary Brown Derby restaurant in Hollywood, Kathy and her family would go there on special occasions. Glamorous and glitzy, the place was an eye-opener for a twelve-year-old girl who was amazed to be sitting near the biggest movie stars in the world. Nobody asked the stars for a selfie back then; instead, Kathy wondered, what were they having for dinner? Many of them had the Cobb Salad, which was prepared by waiters who would make the French dressing tableside, then pour and present the salad to their enraptured diners.

This is Kathy's updated, even more California-y version of that California classic.

Make sure your guests get a look at the military precision with which you've laid out the rows, then add the dressing and mix the whole salad, and you're transported back to the 1960s Brown Derby, where you whisper to your kids, "That woman in the corner is Judy Garland," to which they will respond, "Who's Judy Garland?"

1 envelope Hidden Valley ranch salad
    dressing
1 cup milk
1 cup mayonnaise (Duke's is our favorite)
Sriracha (optional)
½ head iceberg lettuce
1 head romaine lettuce
1 bunch fresh arugula
½ red onion, cut into medium dice
2 medium tomatoes, seeded and cut into
    medium dice
2 cups cubed (¾-inch) cooked chicken
    breast

2 avocados, pitted, peeled, and cut into
    ½-inch cubes
2 cups cooked corn kernels (from 3 ears
    fresh corn if in season)
3 hard-boiled eggs, thinly sliced
½ cup crumbled blue cheese
8 slices bacon, cooked until crisp and
    coarsely chopped

1. Place a large salad bowl in the refrigerator or freezer.

2. Prepare the salad dressing according to the package directions using the milk and mayo (if you're a Sriracha fan, add as much as you like to give it some extra zip). Set the dressing aside in the refrigerator.

3. This salad is all about the wow factor when your diners see all of the various ingredients lined up in pretty rows. First, finely chop the lettuces. This isn't like lettuce in a regular salad—think *really* chopped, almost minced. Place the greens in the bottom of the chilled salad bowl, add the red onion, and toss together. Smooth the top of the lettuces to make an even surface.

4. The most important step! Evenly arrange all of the other ingredients in rows over the lettuces. We start with the bright red tomatoes down the center of the bowl, then arrange the other ingredients outward from the tomatoes in the straightest rows possible.

5. Bring the salad to the table to show it off, slather on the dressing, toss well, and serve.

FULLY LOADED WEDGE SALAD

Whenever we celebrate with a night out on the town, we always order a wedge salad. But we've grown past iceberg lettuce and replaced that green bowling ball with a crisp romaine heart. This version of Grandma's buttermilk dressing recipe is super simple (and you can even swap out the homemade dressing for a bottle of ranch or blue cheese if you're rushed for time).

This salad just screams, *"Yes, I'm eating cheese and bacon on a salad, What's it to ya?"*

DRESSING
⅓ cup mayonnaise (Duke's is our favorite)
¾ cup sour cream
½ teaspoon garlic powder
½ teaspoon freshly ground black pepper
¼ teaspoon Worcestershire sauce
2 to 3 tablespoons milk
¼ cup crumbled blue cheese

SALADS
2 romaine hearts
12 ounces grape tomatoes, halved

4 slices bacon, cooked until crisp and crumbled
Chopped chives or green onions (green tops only), for garnish

1. To make the dressing: In a medium bowl, combine the mayo, sour cream, garlic powder, pepper, and Worcestershire sauce. Add enough milk to thin it down, then stir in the blue cheese. Taste and adjust the seasonings. Set aside.
2. To prepare the salads: Wash the romaine hearts and remove any imperfect leaves. You can trim a bit off the stem end for cosmetic reasons, but leave it mostly intact so that it holds the leaves together. Halve each heart lengthwise and place one half on each of four serving plates. Divide the tomatoes among the plates, then pour the dressing over the lettuce. Crumble the bacon on top and garnish with a few chopped chives to serve.

SIDES

ON THE RADIO KATHY HEARD AN INTER-view with a single-parent mother whose three kids had all received perfect SAT scores and been admitted to Ivy League schools. The interviewer asked, "What's your secret?" She gave him an answer he wasn't expecting.

"For the last five years, I've been making them fish for breakfast."

That was all Kathy had to hear. She sprang into action, went to Costco, and bought a big bag of whitefish. That next morning by 7:15 a.m. the fish was steamed and plated, ready to turn our three small kids into geniuses.

"If I eat that, can I get an Eggo, too?" Peter's negotiation didn't work, and twenty awkward minutes later, not one child had eaten a single bite. As they got in the car, Kathy handed each of them an Eggo, so nobody would question why they were hangry at school.

You're never too old for a bib.

The next morning, the kids came downstairs, and the fish was again waiting.

"Come on, try it . . . please?"

They sat and stared at it until Sally started crying, then Mary blurted out, "If we have to eat fish for breakfast, I don't want to go to college!"

And with that, Kathy's brave experiment in feeding their way to a Harvard admission failed.

It was but a speed bump in our parenting journey, as we tried to introduce the kids not only to good healthy foods but also to interesting dishes on our travels.

Once, along La Rambla in Barcelona, we decided to try tapas. They were so beautiful in the display case, but something got lost in translation and the waiter brought us a complete order of dishes that looked like props from a Tim Burton movie. The fish tapas were served with the eyes still intact, so they could watch us as we ate them. Thankfully we could close *our* eyes, and there was room-temperature white wine to wash it down.

Meanwhile, on a cruise around the Caribbean, a high-school-age Peter Doocy ordered sweetbreads off the menu, thinking it sounded like Cinnamon Toast Crunch. When it arrived he was horrified to discover it was not cereal, but lamb glands. To prove to his sisters that he was either a gourmand or a human garbage can, he ate it all. Then retired to his stateroom for the rest of the day.

On another family vacation with my in-laws, Rob and Gwen, we took the entire family to a very fancy Rocky Mountain restaurant accessible only by sleigh. When Gwen made the reservation, the restaurant made it clear that they did welcome children, but they would have to order off the regular menu.

"Do you have pasta?"

"Yes."

Perfect.

When we arrived we were expecting a penne or linguine, but the only pasta on the menu was sage butternut squash gnocchi. What three-year-old is going to eat that?

"Can you leave the sage sauce off the gnocchi?" we asked.

"No, it has to come out of the kitchen exactly as the chef envisioned it," the waiter told us, although we knew he was lying. It was also $38—in 1998! Sally ate exactly half of one gnoccho and spit it out. Peter ate her leftovers.

The only time Peter declined to eat an exotic food was on a college tour of the Middle East. Somewhere in Egypt, the tour group ate at a place that would flunk a health department inspection, and Peter contracted a ferocious case of *C. diff*. While everyone else was sampling *shawarma*, *fatteh*, and *kushari*, the only thing his inflamed colon would allow him to down was a cheeseburger at the Nile Hilton in Cairo.

He'd walk a mile for a cheeseburger.

On the plus side, he lost his freshman fifteen in four days.

What was the big lesson of those Wonder Years of parenting? Simply put, kids are going to eat what kids are going to eat.

PERFECT POTATO SALAD

•MAKES 12 SERVINGS•

The first time Kathy made a potato salad, it was from a fancy cookbook and it took her most of the day to prepare. Having grown up helping my mom make her potato salad with Miracle Whip and French's mustard, I knew what it should look like when it's served . . . with paprika. *Shake, shake, shake!*

When Kathy saw that smear of red across her masterpiece, I can honestly say I don't think I've seen her angrier. I'm sure at that moment she was trying to remember why she didn't marry that nice baseball player from Kansas City.

Three decades later, she has developed her own personal potato salad that is fast, easy, and so delicious. It's a happy side dish to any summertime meal, as long as nobody mentions the unauthorized paprika scandal of 1986.

24 small red potatoes
Salt
10 hard-boiled eggs, peeled and cut into medium dice
2 large carrots, grated
4 large celery stalks, cut into medium dice
6 green onions, thinly sliced
6 tablespoons chopped fresh dill
1 teaspoon freshly ground black pepper
1½ cups sour cream
½ cup mayonnaise (Duke's is our favorite)
3 tablespoons Dijon mustard

1. Place the potatoes in a large pot of salted water and bring it to a boil over medium-high heat. Cook until the potatoes are almost tender, 12 to 15 minutes. Drain the potatoes, let them cool, and cut them into quarters.

2. In a large serving bowl, combine the potatoes, eggs, carrots, celery, green onions, most of the dill (save a sprinkle for garnishing), 1 teaspoon salt, and the pepper and stir gently to combine.

3. In a small bowl, mix the sour cream, mayo, and mustard. Add it to the potato mixture and mix thoroughly.

4. Garnish with the reserved dill and refrigerate until it's time to eat.

MAPLE-BACON ROASTED BRUSSELS SPROUTS

This is our go-to side dish for fall and wintertime suppers. Not only is it delicious, but the hot oven also warms the kitchen and makes the whole house smell like maple and bacon. You'll think you're at Larry the Cable Guy's house. What's better than that? Okay, winning the Powerball is better, but this is something you can count on.

> 2 pounds Brussels sprouts, ends trimmed, halved
> ¼ cup extra-virgin olive oil
> Salt and freshly ground black pepper
> 6 slices thick-cut bacon
> ⅓ cup pure maple syrup
> 3 tablespoons butter

1. Preheat the oven to 400°F.
2. In a large bowl, combine the Brussels sprouts, olive oil, and salt and pepper to taste.
3. Place the sprouts cut side down on a rimmed baking sheet and roast for 20 minutes. Flip them over and roast until tender, about 15 minutes longer.
4. Meanwhile, place the bacon on a separate baking sheet and bake for 15 minutes. Remove from the oven and carefully brush with the maple syrup. Return to the oven and bake about 5 minutes more, until the bacon is cooked and the maple syrup is sizzling. Set the bacon on a plate to cool (not on paper towels; the bacon will stick to them). When the bacon is cool, chop it into ¾-inch pieces. Set aside.
5. In a small saucepan, melt the butter over low heat. Stir in 3 tablespoons of the maple syrup and quickly remove the pan from the heat.
6. Remove the Brussels sprouts from the oven (but leave the oven on). Scrape the Brussels sprouts into a large bowl, add the bacon, and pour the warm syrup mixture over the top. Give a good stir.
7. Return the sprout mixture to the baking sheet and bake for a few minutes, long enough to make it greatly gooier.
8. Transfer the sprouts to a serving bowl, serve, and enjoy.

PEANUT BUTTER PASTA

This was a landmark dish. It was the first time our kids actually liked something that wasn't a member of the chicken finger family, and as it turns out it was actually approaching foreign cuisine.

If you said, "Kids, tonight we're having Chinese noodles," nobody would come to the table—they'd order a pizza on their flip phones and have it delivered by ladder to the second floor. So instead we always called it "peanut butter pasta." Thankfully, the kids were too distracted by their Game Boys to question the name.

PEANUT BUTTER SAUCE
½ cup creamy peanut butter
⅓ cup hot water
1 garlic clove, crushed through a garlic press
2 teaspoons grated fresh ginger
1 tablespoon honey
¼ teaspoon red pepper flakes
¼ cup tamari

PASTA
½ pound spaghetti
Salt

3 green onions, green tops only, thinly sliced for garnish (optional)
Peanuts, for garnish (optional)

1. To make the peanut butter sauce: In a blender, combine the sauce ingredients. Blend on low speed and increase the speed until the sauce is super smooth; about 2 minutes works great. You'll probably have to stop and use a spatula to scrape the peanut butter off the sides once or twice.

2. To prepare the pasta: Cook the spaghetti in salted water according to the package directions. Drain and run the noodles under cold water to stop the cooking.

3. Drain the noodles and place them in a serving bowl. Add the peanut butter sauce and toss to coat.

4. If desired, garnish with a sprinkling of green onions and/or peanuts and serve.

PESTO GRILLED CORN

When people find out that I was raised in Kansas, they say one of two things: "Dorothy, you're not in Kansas anymore . . ." or "Kansas . . . that's the corn state, right?" No, Kansas is the *wheat* state and *Iowa* is the corn state. Luckily I was born in Iowa, so I never take offense. *The Wizard of Oz* thing does bug me, but imagine how Dr. Oz feels. You can never turn that off.

Anyway, in the summer, we eat a lot of fresh corn, and we discovered a great variation one night when I plopped down the just-grilled corn on a serving plate still covered in pesto. We ate it and realized they were perfect together. This reminds me of that famous 1980s TV commercial where the girl walking down the street with an open jar of peanut butter collides with the guy walking with the chocolate and after they yell at each other they realize they've just created Reese's Peanut Butter Cups!

Our discovery is just like that . . . except with pesto.

6 ears corn, unhusked
½ cup store-bought pesto (we use Costco's Kirkland brand)
Grated Parmesan cheese, for garnish
Red pepper flakes (optional)

1. Preheat a grill to high heat.

2. Place the corn directly on the grill, with the husks intact. Every 5 minutes, turn them to a side that's not yet charred. After all sides are grill marked, about 20 minutes, set the corn aside to cool.

3. Carefully pull back and remove the husks and remove the corn silk. If you want grill marks, return the cobs to the grill for a couple minutes. It won't take long.

4. Brush the pesto onto the cobs, top with grated Parmesan, and if you like a little kick, sprinkle on some pepper flakes. Time to eat!

Photo on page 141.

SWEET POTATO–PRALINE CASSEROLE

·MAKES 6 SERVINGS·

Over the course of a family's life, people change, and so do their recipes. This is one of them.

When the kids were young, they loved sweet potato casserole, or rather they scraped the marshmallows off the top, which they adored, and left the orange stuff untouched. So we started to minimize the fluffy top, going from the large marshmallows to the minis, and by their late teens, we made it with no topping. Progress!

After many family holidays in Georgia and South Carolina, we've added a pecan-y praline crunch on the top, and now the kids start with this on Thanksgiving.

CASEROLE
**4 large sweet potatoes, peeled and cut into
    1-inch cubes**
⅓ cup milk
4 tablespoons (½ stick) butter, melted
2 large eggs, lightly beaten
¼ cup pure maple syrup
½ teaspoon salt
1 teaspoon pure vanilla extract

PECAN TOPPING
1¼ cups chopped pecans
1 cup packed light brown sugar
½ cup flour
4 tablespoons (½ stick) butter, melted

1. Preheat the oven to 350°F. Grease a 9 x 13-inch baking dish.

2. To make the casserole: Place the sweet potatoes in a large pot, add water to cover, and bring to a boil over medium-high heat. Reduce the heat to a simmer and cook until tender, 15 to 20 minutes. Drain and set aside.

3. Place the sweet potatoes in a stand mixer and whip them until smooth. Add the milk, melted butter, eggs, maple syrup, salt, and vanilla and beat until completely combined.

4. Pour the mixture into the prepared baking dish, smooth out the top evenly, and bake for 30 minutes.

5. Meanwhile, make the pecan topping: In a medium bowl, combine the pecans, brown sugar, flour, and melted butter.

6. Remove the baking dish from the oven. Sprinkle the pecan mixture evenly over the baked sweet potatoes, then return to the oven and bake until golden, 5 to 10 minutes. Let the sweet potatoes rest for 20 minutes before serving—they will be hot!

GREEN BEANS AND GOAT CHEESE

One summer growing up the only thing that grew in our garden was green beans. My dad planted so many that my mom wound up serving them at every meal, then canned twenty mason jars of them that we ate through the next year. I hated them and promised I would never eat them again. *Ever.*

Forty years later, I love 'em!

Given the nostalgic way our minds work, they remind me of that happy time growing up on the farm when we actually grew our food out back. We were Whole Foods before Whole Foods.

¼ cup chopped pecans or walnuts
1 pound green beans, ends trimmed
¼ cup extra-virgin olive oil
2 tablespoons balsamic vinegar
1 garlic clove, minced
1 medium shallot, thinly sliced
Salt and freshly ground black pepper
1 cup grape or cherry tomatoes, halved
½ cup crumbled goat cheese
1 tablespoon balsamic glaze, for garnish

1. In a small nonstick skillet, toast the nuts over medium-high heat. It takes only a couple minutes, so watch them carefully. Set aside. Okay, eat one, they're delicious.

2. Bring a large pot of water to a boil and cook the beans until they are tender-crisp, 5 to 8 minutes. Drain and place in a bowl of cold water.

3. To make the dressing, in a small bowl, stir the olive oil, vinegar, garlic, and shallot. Add a shake of salt and pepper and whisk well.

4. Drain the beans and place in a serving bowl. Add the tomatoes and dressing and give a good stir to coat everything. Just before serving, toss in the goat cheese and nuts. Squirt the balsamic glaze on top in a zigzag fashion.

Photo on page 123.

BUFFALO HASSELBACK POTATOES

When I described these potatoes to Elisabeth Hasselbeck, my former cohost on *Fox & Friends*, she wondered first if they were gluten-free, and then if she was related to them. Turns out that Hasselback potatoes are from Sweden, not a famous TV and football family.

Just like my daughter Mary, the Hasselbecks (Tim and Elisabeth) went to Boston College where we observed that most BC students, seem to consume their body weight in hot sauce. I guess it keeps them warm on those frosty nights along the Charles River when they are supposed to be studying in the library.

Hasselback potatoes are kind of complicated, so we're making this recipe much easier, using the microwave to speed things up so you're less likely to have underdone potatoes after an hour of baking. So if you like Buffalo sauce and buttery potatoes . . . then this spud's for you.

4 medium russet potatoes, scrubbed
8 tablespoons (1 stick) butter, melted
   (more if needed)
Kosher salt and freshly ground black pepper
¼ cup Frank's RedHot Original Cayenne
   Pepper sauce
¼ cup grated Cheddar cheese
⅓ cup sour cream
1 tablespoon half-and-half or whole milk
¼ cup crumbled blue cheese
2 green onions, sliced, for garnish

1. Preheat the oven to 400°F.

2. Stab the potatoes a couple times and then microwave them until cooked through, 10 to 12 minutes, depending on your microwave's intensity. Wrap the potatoes in foil and let rest for 10 minutes.

3. Unwrap the potatoes. One at a time, set a potato on a cutting board and place a wooden spoon to either side, so you can't cut through to the board. Make slices across the potato ¼ inch apart (this is wider than a regular Hasselback potato), leaving about 1 inch at each end. The potatoes are very soft; cut gently so you don't rip the skin.

4. Set the potatoes in a baking dish and pour half the melted butter down between as many slices as you can. Sprinkle on salt and pepper to taste and bake for 20 minutes. Remove the dish from the oven and baste with most of the remaining butter (leave 1 tablespoon in the bowl). Whisk the Frank's RedHot sauce with the remaining butter, then drizzle it over the potatoes and between as many slices as possible. Bake for 10 minutes, then remove from the oven and sprinkle the potatoes with the Cheddar. Pop the pan back in the oven for 5 minutes to melt the cheese.

5. In a small bowl, combine the sour cream, half-and-half, and blue cheese. Add salt and pepper to taste and slather the mixture on top of the spuds. Garnish with the green onions and serve.

BOW TIE PESTO

When we moved to New Jersey, we discovered it's not just the Garden State, it's the also Pasta State. In Virginia, we'd mainly just boil the kids spaghetti, but once we arrived in Jersey, the kids started demanding new pasta shapes. Alphabet letters, wagon wheels, butterflies, or bow ties—it wasn't just dinner; it was a scavenger hunt with red sauce.

As the kids got older, their tastes in sauces changed, but their love of shapes did not, and this is one of Peter's favorites. And as a bonus, the bow tie reminds us of the bow tie he wore for his job at the fancy grocery store.

1 cup fresh basil leaves, washed, plus more for garnish
2 garlic cloves, peeled
3 tablespoons pine nuts
¼ cup freshly grated Parmesan cheese
½ teaspoon salt, plus more for the boiling water
¼ teaspoon freshly ground black pepper

¼ cup extra-virgin olive oil
½ pound bow tie pasta
1 pint cherry or grape tomatoes
¼ teaspoon red pepper flakes
4 ounces goat cheese

1. In a food processor, combine the basil, garlic, pine nuts, Parmesan, salt, and pepper. Pulse to combine and stream in the olive oil until the mixture is finely chopped but not totally pureed. Set the pesto aside.

2. Cook the pasta in boiling salted water according to the package directions. Reserving ¼ cup of the pasta water, drain the pasta and return it to the pot. Add the pesto, tomatoes, pepper flakes, a little more than half of the goat cheese, and the reserved pasta water and give it a good stir to melt the cheese.

3. Top with the remaining goat cheese, garnish with basil leaves, and serve.

PETER'S POTATOES

• MAKES 8 SERVINGS •

Everybody loves potatoes. One time I was having lunch with one of America's most famous physicians at Michael's in New York. I ordered a chicken paillard that was served with a golden mountain of French fries. The good doctor ordered a very responsible and healthy salad. That very day his diet book was number one in America, and of course everybody at the other tables was looking to see what he was eating . . . because that meant it was good for you.

About ten minutes after our lunches were served, he whispered, "Is anybody looking at us?" and I said, "No, why?" and with that he plucked two fries off my plate. Down the hatch they went.

"Thank you," he said, and we continued our conversation as I thought, *Boy, am I glad I didn't invent the _____ Diet—I'd starve!* Dr. _____ could eat as many of my fries as he wanted, he picked up the check.

My son, Peter, loves these potatoes (too much butter for the doctor), and over the years we've tweaked this simple recipe, which originated with my mom. Today I'll sometimes make this as a predinner appetizer while preparing a big meal and pull the tray out of the oven and have something for the kids to graze on while they pretend they can't hear me asking them to take out the recycling.

½ stick butter or ¼ cup extra-virgin olive oil
4 large russet potatoes
Kosher salt and freshly ground black pepper
1 tablespoon herbes de Provence
Grated Parmesan cheese, for garnish

1. Preheat the oven to 425°F.

2. Either run the half stick of butter over a large baking sheet to butter the pan or brush the pan with olive oil, your choice.

3. Peel the potatoes, then slice the potatoes as thinly as you can; if you have a mandoline, that works best. Just be careful to hold off on that glass of wine until after you've cut the potatoes. If you've got a food processor, that'll make quick work when you use the slicing disk.

4. Take the slices from about half a potato and arrange them in a short row of overlapping layers on the baking sheet, each piece slightly overlapped by ½ inch or so from the first, so they look like a short row of scalloped potatoes (without the cream sauce). My kids sometimes arrange them fanned out like a deck of cards and call them *poker potatoes*. Don't know where they got that; they weren't raised in Vegas, baby.

5. Give the potatoes a shake of salt, then melt the butter and dribble it on each line of potatoes. Use a brush to evenly distribute the butter. Lightly sprinkle with pepper.

6. Bake until the potatoes on the edges are deep brown and the rest turn golden, at least 30 minutes. The timing really depends upon how thickly you've sliced them. The first and last ones in every line will brown first, so watch that they don't overcook. If they brown too early and it's freaking you out, use a strip of foil to cover that section of the spuds.

7. In the last 5 minutes of baking, sprinkle on the herbes de Provence and Parmesan. Serve each diner their own row of potatoes. These are best warm.

JERSEY CORN RAVIOLI

This is our favorite homemade summertime pasta. Our friend Kevin Kohler, the owner and chef at Café Panache in Ramsey, New Jersey (which we regard as the best around), makes his official restaurant version with homemade pasta dough, but that takes a lot of time for a home cook like me who could be spending that time looking at cat videos on his phone. So to make it easier, we substitute wonton wrappers, which work great.

Kevin serves this as both an appetizer and an entrée. I like it so much that I'd have it for dessert.

1 cup heavy cream
2 teaspoons polenta
1 teaspoon freshly grated nutmeg (about ½ nut)
Kernels from 4 cooked ears fresh corn
One 12-ounce package wonton wrappers (40 wrappers makes 20 ravioli)
Salt
10 tablespoons + 2 teaspoons (1⅓ sticks) butter
Shaved pecorino cheese or popcorn, for garnish

1. In a medium saucepan, combine the cream, polenta, nutmeg, and corn. Bring to a simmer over medium heat and cook for 5 minutes until completely heated, stirring occasionally.

2. Pour the mixture into a food processor and process until nice and smooth. If too thick, strain through a fine-mesh strainer or sieve. Place the puree in a medium bowl, cover with plastic wrap, and refrigerate it for a few hours to set up.

3. Lay out a wonton wrapper and place about a teaspoonful of the corn mixture in the center. Dip your finger in a small bowl of water and wet the outside edge of the wonton. Place another wonton wrapper on top, press out any air pockets, and squeeze the seams together. Repeat to make the rest of the ravioli.

4. Bring a pot of salted water to a boil. Cook the ravioli a few at a time, until softened and warmed through, 1 or 2 minutes. Reserving ¼ cup of the pasta water, drain the ravioli and set aside.

5. In a large sauté pan, bring the reserved pasta water to a simmer over medium-high heat. Reduce the temperature to medium, add the butter, and let it melt. When the melted butter has thickened a little, add the cooked ravioli a few at a time and sauté to warm them up and coat in the butter.

6. Serve immediately with a garnish of shaved pecorino, or if you want to be really clever, some popcorn.

Photo on page 119.

MUFFIN PAN POTATOES

This became a family favorite after one of our kids (whose identity we shall not reveal) heard Kathy ask me, "Do you know where's the muffin pan?"

That prompted them to start singing with tortured lyrics, "Do you know the Muffin Pan, the Muffin Pan, the Muffin Pan . . . do you know the Muffin Pan who lives on Drury Lane?"

We didn't.

These are easy to make, delicious, and a perfect accompaniment to a nice dinner that needs a potato. And don't they all?

Cooking spray
4 tablespoons (½ stick) butter
3 tablespoons extra-virgin olive oil
2 teaspoons finely chopped fresh rosemary, plus a little more for garnish
1 teaspoon sea salt
½ teaspoon freshly ground black pepper
4 Yukon Gold potatoes, preferably large but long

1. Preheat the oven to 375°F. Coat the cups of a muffin tin with cooking spray.

2. In a glass pie plate, melt the butter in the microwave, then add the olive oil, rosemary, salt, and pepper. Give a stir and set aside.

3. Peel the potatoes and stand them upright to see if they will fit inside a muffin tin well. If needed, cut off some of the width so that they will fit, then slice the potatoes crosswise with a knife or a mandoline set to 1/16 to 1/8 inch thick. Place the potatoes in the melted butter mixture and mix gently to lightly coat them.

4. Distribute the potatoes evenly so that each muffin cup has an equal amount of potatoes. Pour any leftover butter mixture over the potatoes; toss a pinch of rosemary on top.

5. Bake until tender, bubbling, and golden, 50 to 60 minutes.

6. Run a knife around each potato stack and use a serving spoon to fish it out of the muffin tin

Photo on page 147.

5

SANDWICHES AND BREADS

OUR KIDS GREW UP ON SANDWICHES and really good bread. New Jersey is a great place for both.

When Peter was a freshman in high school, he landed a job at the fanciest grocery store we'd ever seen: the Market Basket in Franklin Lakes, New Jersey, which pioneered the idea of ready-to-eat foods that were easy for suburban commuters to just grab and go. It was also the most high-end joint we'd ever seen.

"I didn't realize Rolex made a margarine. . . ."

A whole store of fabulous foodstuffs from all over the globe—air-dried and cold-smoked Italian sausages, live Maine lobsters near the Kobe beef, imported cheeses and olive oils—it was a collection of the most beautiful foods for sale in America. This store was so swanky that while Peter was hired as a stock *boy*, we called him a stock *analyst*.

The clientele ranged from famous NFL players and movie stars to CEOs and captains of industry. Our daughter Mary later worked there as a cashier, heard the crazy things people from New Jersey say to clerks, and turned the stories into a college entrance essay, which got her accepted into the Ivy League. My favorite story Mary told was of the Fortune 500 CEO who insisted that she manually enter the prices into the cash register one at a time and not use the checkout scanner, because that would make the food radioactive.

Working the aisles as a stock *analyst*, shoppers would see Peter's professional attire, a pressed white shirt and black bow tie, and ask him where things were located and then advice on *what* to buy. Peter got proficient in pasta shapes and uses: "My mom uses tagliatelle for that cream sauce," he'd suggest to suburban dads who'd dashed in for a pound of noodles. He was good at identifying and pointing in the direction of everything but produce. To Peter, any green thing—tarragon, cilantro, dill, arugula—was an indistinguishable weed. One day a shopper flagged down Peter, pointed at an item on his list, and said "I need this . . ." without saying what *it* was. *It* was something Peter had never seen on a shopping list before.

Stumped, Peter finally asked the manager, "Hey, Phil, where's the *anus*?"

Phil, who had been around the produce block before, looked at the shopper's list and with a grin told Peter he was mispronouncing *anise*. It was in produce.

Peter kept that job through college, because he really wanted to make his own money, so why not work at a store that sells Chihuahua-size shrimp for $39 a pound? Peter was learning the true value of a dollar, and at that store a dollar bought $\frac{1}{39}$th of a pound of shrimp.

While Kathy and I largely taught ourselves to cook, we did both attend cooking school . . . for one night. Our friend Todd bought his wife Madeline a four-person cooking class for her birthday, and they invited us to join them. A professional chef showed us how to make a delicious chicken recipe that we pledged to make again, but never did. (We've observed that when you're drinking wine, you make big plans that you quickly forget about the next day.) Right next to where Kathy was sitting during the lesson was a beautiful display of cake domes.

"I think I want one of those," she said in my direction, but I pretended not to hear (we didn't have one square inch of extra kitchen space). But Madeline had heard, and the next day she gifted Kathy a crystal cake dome. I told her she'd never use it. Kathy wanted to prove me wrong, and in retrospect it was one of the best things she ever did.

"What's in the dome?" was the first thing the kids would ask when they rushed in after school. Usually it was a cake or a pie. Always stocked, it became a neighborhood attraction. For variety I bought her a second dome, which challenged her to keep two domes stocked simultaneously—and she did, for years.

We are a typical family—Kathy does almost all cooking indoors and I do most of the grilling outside. One night I made myself a bet that I could make an entire meal and *fill the dome*, and do it all on our Weber grill. The idea was to never dirty a single pot or pan.

Life needs more barbecue.

"Mommy! Daddy's baking brownies on the barbecue!" our youngest announced to my wife, who then started a clock in her head until I admitted that brownies and grills don't mix.

The chicken, rosemary potatoes, blue cheese bread, and corn on the cob were easy, and the brownies would be a culinary showstopper that our family would talk about for years to come, I just knew it.

"They're perfect!" I announced as I waved the brownie pan (the only pan I used) under the nose of my wife, who seemed genuinely delighted. Once they'd cooled down, I started to cut them into squares, but the knife would not go any deeper than about half an inch. Apparently Duncan Hines's kitchen technicians had meant it when they called for a conventional oven, not an outdoor furnace. The brownie top looked perfect, but the bottom of the pan, closest to the 75,000 BTUs, had fused and melted together into a 9 x 13-inch briquette.

Flop sweat beading on my forehead, I remembered that we'd bought a specialty knife we saw on TV that could be used to cut beer cans and rain gutters. Retrieving it from the pile of other never-used miracle products, I was able to cut about a dozen 2-inch brownie squares that were soft on the top and concrete on the bottom. Next, my plan was to essentially fillet each brownie, cutting the soft top from the rock-hard bottom. And that's exactly what I did on two brownies. On the third I used too much pressure on a part I thought was hard but was actually soft, and the knife flew out of the brownie and into my hand. It took about a second for my brain to process the fact that I'd just *cut off my fingertip!*

With blood squirting everywhere, Monty Python style, my wife calmly told me to go to the ER.

But I was the bullhead who hadn't yet met his deductible for the year, so I bandaged and Neosporined my finger and ten minutes later returned to the blood-spattered table. One of my joker kids used driveway chalk to draw a murder victim outline around the brownie pan. They watched too much TV back then.

While I triaged myself, Kathy had served the dinner, so returning to the table I laid the two perfectly carved brownie squares on a paper plate for dessert. They looked blood-free to me.

"Dad, you can't make us eat them. . . ."

And nobody did, except me. My brownie was baked to a tasty O-negative, without a doubt the most painful dessert I'd ever created.

I can laugh about it now, because it's a true story from our family's history. All the kids remember it as if it were yesterday, because shared family experiences around the grill or the stove or dinner table are the things they'll remember the rest of their lives.

The hardest part of cooking for our family has been the fact that our kids grew up. They went from fussy eaters, to big eaters, to college kids (who wanted Buffalo sauce on everything), and now they've graduated from us and live somewhere else.

The nights of our big noisy family meals are over, but thankfully a couple times a year we're all able to get together and I'll make them Egg in a Nest for breakfast and Kathy will roast the peppers for her red pepper pasta.

Family life comes and goes in phases, and right now we're at the stage where it's just Kathy and me, waiting for the kids to return home.

The dome is empty, but Kathy can have a cake in there in an hour.

BABY BLT

When we lived outside Washington, DC, one year, I was often jolted awake around 2:30 in the morning to some kind of urgent alarm going off. The first fifty times I'd race downstairs to find . . . my pregnant wife, microwaving bacon in our Amana Radarange for a BLT.

Second and third trimesters. Kathy craved bacon.

We still make these—after all, she made them throughout her pregnancies and the kids all turned out fine. At that time, we joked we should name that child Oscar, as in Oscar Mayer, but upon delivery we could not name a blood relative after something from the bacon family. Sorry, Kevin.

Kathy loved to eat BLTs with a pickle slice when she was pregnant, so now when she reaches for the jar of Vlasics, it still sends a shudder down my spine. I'll ask her, "Are you . . ."

And she'll answer, "Yes, I am . . . hungry."

They make a good pickle.

8 slices thick-cut bacon
Pure maple syrup
¼ cup good-quality mayonnaise (Duke's is
    our favorite)
1 tablespoon Dijon mustard
8 slices country bread or sourdough
1 large tomato, cut into slices ½ inch thick
Salt
6 iceberg lettuce leaves

1. Preheat the oven to 400°F. Line a baking sheet with foil.

2. Lay the bacon slices on the lined baking sheet. (You can microwave the bacon and save a step, but frying it up and adding a little maple syrup makes the bacon 37 percent tastier. Trust us.) Bake for 20 minutes, remove from the oven, and brush some maple syrup on each side. Return to the oven, and bake until crispy and delicious, another 5 minutes. Set aside on a plate (not on paper towels; the bacon will stick to the paper, you won't be able to remove it, and you'll wind up with BLTTs: bacon, lettuce, tomato, and towel sandwiches).

3. In a small bowl, combine the mayonnaise and mustard.

4. Now let's assemble the sandwiches. Toast the bread, then spread the mayo mixture over 1 side of each of the 4 top pieces. Place the tomatoes on the bottom toast slices, give a light shake of salt, and add 2 pieces of bacon per sandwich, followed by the crispy lettuce. Close the sandwich with a piece of toasted and mayo'd bread, cut in half, and serve.

CHEESY BIEROCKS

When I was growing up in Kansas, this was a favorite recipe borrowed from our Mennonite neighbors. The story went that fifty years earlier when the farmers were working the fields, their wives would spend the morning making these bierocks, which are a kind of a dough pocket sandwich. Then the bakers would take the bierocks out to the men in the fields for lunch, and they'd eat it with their cleaner hand. This was important back in the days before Purell.

When we lived in Russell, Kansas, my mom started adding cheese, and there was no going back to the original recipe. At our house, we regard this as the original Hot Pocket.

1 pound lean ground beef
1 Vidalia (sweet) onion, cut into medium dice
4 cups coarsely shredded cabbage
⅛ teaspoon garlic powder
4 teaspoons Worcestershire sauce
Salt and freshly ground black pepper
2 rectangular sheets store-bought pizza dough, about 8 x 14 inches (we use Wewalka)
1 cup shredded Cheddar cheese
1 egg, whisked

1. Preheat the oven to 375°F. Grease a large baking sheet.

2. In a large skillet, cook the beef over medium-high heat until it's halfway browned. Add the onion and cook for 3 or 4 minutes, then add the cabbage and cook until the cabbage is softened and the beef is browned and cooked through, about 5 minutes. Add the garlic powder, Worcestershire sauce, and salt and pepper to taste. Simmer until the beef is completely cooked. Set aside.

3. Lay out one rectangular sheet of pizza dough horizontally on a piece of parchment paper. Use a pizza cutter to cut the rectangle of dough into 6 equal squares of about 4 x 4 inches—though the actual dimensions will depend on the dough you buy. We make a single lengthwise cut from left to right, dividing the dough into two long rectangles. Then we cut the remaining dough into thirds, winding up with 6 pieces. This will probably leave you with a little strip of dough on one side. Repeat with the second rectangle of dough for a total of 12 squares.

4. Divide the Cheddar among the squares, placing up to 1 tablespoon of cheese in the center of each. Top the cheese with 2 or 3 tablespoons of the meat mix. Carefully pull up the four corners of the dough, one at a time, and pinch them together to seal the filling within the dough.

5. Place the bierocks, seam side down, on the prepared baking sheet. Brush the tops with the whisked egg.

6. Bake until golden brown, 25 to 30 minutes. Let them rest about 5 minutes before serving.

AVOCADO TOAST

This was the first "Cooking with Friends" recipe ever prepared on the *Fox & Friends* show.

Years earlier I'd read a column in Kathy's *Bon Appétit* magazine by editor in chief Adam Rapoport about how he'd forgotten to plan for an appetizer for guests one night, but he did have some crusty bread and some ripe avocados, so he created an impromptu avocado toast based on something he'd had at a fancy New York restaurant. His guests loved it.

In 2015, when we started the "Cooking with Friends" segment, we invited Adam to show us how he made it. To demonstrate that his recipe was a Doocy family staple, we brought in my younger daughter, Sally, to prove we were avocado toast disciples. Both Doocys and Mr. Rapoport all made avocado toast, and it was very funny TV. After it ran, we got thousands of requests for the recipe, and I'm sure it was unrelated to our TV demonstration, but avocado toast then became a part of the culinary zeitgeist, and *everybody* started making it.

We like to think we started the craze, but really it was Adam the editor, who forgot one night he needed something for dinner guests and had to ad lib an appetizer. Here's our version of the recipe that changed America.

> Good extra-virgin olive oil
> Four ¾-inch-thick slices crusty bread
> 2 garlic cloves
> 1 avocado, pitted and peeled
> Sea salt
> Red pepper flakes

1. Set the oven to broil, with an oven rack about 6 inches below the heat source.

2. Brush olive oil on one side of the bread slices, then place them oil side up on a baking sheet and slide it under the broiler. Because there's oil on it, it could turn golden brown in less than a minute, so watch carefully. (You can also use an outdoor grill; as soon as you get a good grill mark, remove the bread from the heat.) You're only doing one side of the bread.

3. Slice a garlic clove in half and rub it gently over the grilled part of the toast.

4. Cut a few slices of avocado into a fan shape (connected at the end) and place it on one of the bread slices. Smash it into place with a fork so it doesn't fall off when you take your first bite. Drizzle with olive oil, shake on a little sea salt, and top with a shake of red pepper flakes. Repeat to make more avocado toasts. Wow, that's good!

VARIATIONS

The simple version is great, but try these toppings if you want to fancify:

- Bacon (cooked and crumbled), tomato (diced), and balsamic reduction drizzle
- Cucumber, tomato (diced), and feta cheese (crumbled)
- Frank's RedHot sauce drizzle and blue cheese (crumbled)

CAPRESE PANINI

During our much-needed kitchen remodel, when the room was stripped to the studs, the panini maker was one of the only appliances left that we could use. This recipe became a family favorite after a bumper crop of basil in the backyard—I made a fresh batch of pesto at least once a week that year. The following summer, a ferocious family of renegade rabbits that sublet our backyard fell in love with the basil as well, and that ended the basil pesto that we made at home. Now we save time and just buy it from the store. Kirkland basil pesto (from Costco) is our favorite, and the jar says it's from the Liguria region of Italy, which sounds fancy. We like it because it's a big jar and the pesto stays green and fresh for quite a while after you open it.

Long after the kitchen was completed, we would still drag out the panini maker in the summer when the tomatoes were perfect and the basil was beautiful, as the rabbits in the backyard watched us happily laughing on the deck and wished they had a Costco card, too.

1 large beefsteak tomato, cut into four ½-inch-thick slices
Salt
Balsamic vinegar
8 slices country bread or sourdough
½ cup store-bought pesto (we use Costco's Kirkland brand)
One 8-ounce ball fresh mozzarella cheese, cut into four ½-inch-thick slices
8 tablespoons (1 stick) butter, at room temperature
Potato chips, for serving

1. Preheat a panini maker.
2. Place the tomato slices in a shallow dish, salt them lightly, and drizzle them with some of your favorite balsamic vinegar.
3. Place 8 slices of bread in a row and spread 1 tablespoon of pesto evenly over each slice. Lay a slice of tomato on half of the bread slices, followed by a mozzarella slice. Top with the remaining slices of pesto spread bread, pesto side in. Butter the outside of each sandwich evenly.
4. When the panini maker is ready, cook the sandwiches until the bread is toasty and the cheese is melted, working in batches as needed.
5. Cut the sandwiches in half and serve warm, with potato chips as a perfect crunchy complement.

BBQ CHICKEN AND BACON PIZZA

·MAKES 4 SERVINGS·

I remember when I was about seven and a super-exotic restaurant opened up across the street from Kansas Wesleyan University in Salina, Kansas. It was a surprising hit, and people lined up out the door to try this curious cuisine. My dad was the first family member to actually go inside the new Pizza Hut, and he thought it was really great, mainly because they sold beer.

These days we still love pizza, and it turns out it's a great way to use up leftovers. We always have pizza dough in the fridge, and if we have some leftover meat on hand, we'll chop it up, add some sauce, and spread it on the dough. When I smell it baking I'm instantly back at the Salina Pizza Hut, watching those college kids drink their body weight in Coors 3.2 beer.

Back then I wondered why they never got up to use the restroom. As it turns out, they didn't want to lose their place at the bar, because above it they had the only *color TV* in town, and *Bonanza* was about to start. . . .

1 boneless chicken breast, cooked and cut into ½-inch cubes (pulled pork also works)
½ cup barbecue sauce, plus more for serving (we use Gates of Kansas City because it's the closest thing to the sauce they serve in Heaven—at least that's what we're counting on)

One 14.1-ounce package Wewalka Classic Pizza dough
¼ cup shredded Gouda cheese
1¼ cups shredded mozzarella cheese
½ small red onion, thinly sliced
2 slices bacon, cooked
Chopped fresh cilantro, for garnish (optional)

1. Preheat the oven to 400°F convection (or 425°F standard).
2. In a medium bowl, toss the chicken with a couple tablespoons of the barbecue sauce to coat it well.
3. Unroll the packaged pizza dough onto a baking sheet (Wewalka brand has parchment paper already underneath; if you use another brand, coat the pan with cooking spray first). Spread the remaining barbecue sauce where you'd normally put the marinara on a pizza, leaving an inch around the outside uncovered.
4. Sprinkle the Gouda on top, then the mozzarella. Arrange the chicken evenly on top, sprinkle on red onions to your taste, and crumble the bacon on top.
5. Bake until the pizza is golden brown around the edges and the cheese is browning on top, about 10 minutes.
6. To serve, add a couple squirts of barbecue sauce and some chopped cilantro (unless your kids hate it, like mine).

FLAKY HAM AND CHEESE SANDWICHES

Whenever our family would order sandwiches together, most of the time the kids would all get the same thing: ham and cheese on kaiser rolls with a little mayonnaise and mustard. One time, while on vacation in Paris, the kids ordered fancy flaky puff pastry ham and cheese sandwiches at the French version of Subway (I think it was called Le Subway). We've been making our version ever since. It reminds us of that fun summer in France, when we were pretty sure the Parisians were quietly discussing our American food choices and the fact that I was holding on to last year's haircut.

HONEY-MUSTARD SAUCE
½ cup mayonnaise (Duke's is our favorite)
¼ cup Dijon mustard
Dash of salt
¼ cup honey
1 tablespoon distilled white vinegar

SANDWICHES
One 13.2-ounce package Wewalka Puff
    Pastry dough, at room temperature
⅓ pound very thinly sliced Virginia ham
¾ cup shredded Gruyère cheese
Egg wash: 1 egg whisked with 2 tablespoons
    water

1. To make the honey-mustard sauce: In a small bowl, mix the mayo, mustard, salt, honey, and vinegar. Blend until smooth and set aside.
2. To make the sandwiches: On a piece of parchment paper cut to fit on a baking sheet, roll out the puff pastry with a long side facing you (Wewalka brand comes already on a piece of parchment paper). Cut the dough into 6 equal squares: Using a pizza cutter, cut the dough in half lengthwise, dividing the dough into 2 long rectangles. Now make 2 widthwise cuts to give you 6 pieces total—3 on the top row and 3 below. (The exact dimensions of the squares will depend on the brand of puff pastry you are using.)
3. Preheat the oven to 350°F convection (or 375°F standard).
4. Spoon about 2 teaspoons of the honey-mustard sauce onto the center of each square, then spread it to cover as much of the square as you can, leaving a clean border of ¾ inch on all sides. Next, cut the ham into squares that will cover the mustard part, again leaving about ¾ inch of space around the border. Place up to 2 tablespoons of Gruyère on top of each ham slice.
5. Brush the empty ¾-inch borders with the egg wash. Gently pull up a corner of one square and fold it over to form a triangle. Use a fork to crimp the outside edges together and set it on a baking sheet. Repeat with the rest of the squares. Use the remaining egg wash to brush the tops of all the triangles.
6. Transfer the triangles and the parchment paper to a baking sheet. Bake until golden brown and 100 percent puffed up, 16 to 18 minutes. When first out of the oven these sandwiches are super hot (think the surface of the sun, with cheese), so let them cool 5 minutes, then serve with the rest of the honey-mustard sauce. *Magnifique!*

BOB'S BRUSCHETTA

·MAKES 12 SERVINGS·

One night our friend Bob, a TV producer I'd worked with at NBC and Fox, came over for dinner, just as I was about to warm up the grocery store–bought garlic bread that we always made back then. You know what bread I'm talking about—that baguette wrapped in a foil bag kept in the baskets by the bakery department. With a concerned look, Bob said, "Do you have any idea what's in that?" and I answered, "Yes!" Of course I had no idea what was in it, other than garlic butter and probably more stuff that tastes like garlicky butter.

"Read the bag," Bob said, and I did and was shocked at how mysterious it was.

Bob said, "I don't eat that stuff. You got a tomato?" We nodded yes, and Bob then volunteered, "Let me make you bruschetta."

Great, what's *bruschetta*?

Bob's bruschetta was a lot healthier than the bread in the bag, and thanks to Bob rubbing raw garlic on the toasted bread, it was just as garlicky as the store-bought garlic bread. We now make it two or three times a week during the summer, when the tomatoes are ripest and talented friends are available to come over and cook for us.

1 large or 2 medium perfect summertime tomatoes, seeded and diced
¼ pound fresh mozzarella cheese, cut into ½-inch cubes
Extra-virgin olive oil
1 long thin bread loaf, such as a baguette or Italian loaf
2 or 3 garlic cloves, halved
Basil leaves, for garnish
Sea salt

1. Preheat a grill.

2. In a medium bowl, combine the tomatoes, mozzarella, and a drizzle of olive oil. Set aside.

3. Cut 12 slices of bread, each about ¾ inch thick. Brush one side of each with olive oil and place the slices oiled side down on the hot grill. Remove them quickly once there's a good grill mark—they burn fast!

4. Rub the grilled side of the bread slices with garlic. The garlic will disappear quickly, so have a couple cloves ready as backup.

5. Place the slices grilled side up on a serving platter and scoop 1 or 2 tablespoons of the tomato-mozzarella mixture onto each slice. Garnish with shredded basil, drizzle on a little extra-virgin olive oil, and give a light shake of sea salt across everything before serving.

BUFFALO BLUE BAGUETTE

When Kathy and I were first married, almost every meal showcased a green salad and a long piece of bread. One day while waiting in the Safeway checkout line, Kathy was reading one of those little cookbooks by the cashier and saw a simple bread recipe that reminded her of something, and she concocted this recipe on the spot:

*Buffalo sauce + blue cheese + crusty baguette =
Buffalo blue baguette*

She pulled her cart out of the line, went back into the aisles, and bought some blue cheese. Thirty years later, we're still loving this recipe, grateful that on that day she looked at the little cookbooks and skipped the *National Enquirer* issue featuring top-secret *Dallas* photos of J. R. Ewing in prison.

1 crusty baguette
3 tablespoons butter, at room temperature
3 ounces cream cheese, at room
   temperature
½ cup crumbled blue cheese
Frank's RedHot sauce (or your favorite hot
   sauce)
2 green onions, thinly sliced
Extra-virgin olive oil
Grated Parmesan cheese

1. Preheat the oven to 400°F.
2. Split the bread horizontally in half lengthwise.
3. In a medium bowl, mix together the butter, cream cheese, and blue cheese until well blended. Spread half of the mixture on each of the cut sides of the bread. Splash as much hot sauce as you like over the mixture, then sprinkle with the green onions. Place the bread slices back together, brush the top with olive oil, and sprinkle some Parmesan on top. Wrap the loaf in foil and bake until hot, about 15 minutes.
4. Unwrap the loaf and let it sit for a couple of minutes. It's hot!
5. Slice into 1-inch-thick pieces and serve

PETER'S CHICKEN PARMESAN SLIDERS

A while ago, we went to an Italian restaurant and a strange thing happened—Peter picked up the menu and started eyeballing the entrées. "What are you doing?" I asked.

Peter responded, "You're right." He turned to the waiter and said, "I'll have the chicken Parm."

Chicken Parmesan is Peter's favorite meal—you can take that to the bank. While the rest of the family loves it, the giant portions can be overwhelming, so at my daughter's suggestion we started making a more portable and petite version that has become a family favorite. This is lighter because the chicken is baked, not fried, and we like that it combines the taste of chicken Parmesan with an easy version of our favorite Italian bread, the garlic knot.

GARLIC BISCUITS
3 garlic cloves, minced
2 tablespoons butter
1 tablespoon extra-virgin olive oil
2 teaspoons fresh flat-leaf parsley, finely
   minced
1 can Pillsbury Grands Flaky Layers Original
   biscuits

CHICKEN PARM
2 large eggs
½ cup milk
½ teaspoon salt
¼ teaspoon freshly ground black pepper
1 cup Italian-style dried bread crumbs
4 thin-sliced chicken breasts
Cooking spray
1 cup your favorite marinara sauce, warmed
8 slices packaged mozzarella cheese

1. Preheat the oven to 350°F.
2. To make the garlic biscuits: In a small microwave-safe bowl, combine the garlic, butter, and olive oil and microwave until the butter is melted. Stir in the parsley and set aside.
3. Make the biscuits according to the package directions, but before baking, paint the top of each biscuit with the garlic-butter mixture. Bake until golden brown and set aside in a warm place. (Leave the oven on for the chicken.)
4. To prepare the chicken Parm: In two shallow bowls, make a breading assembly line. Whisk together the egg, milk, salt, and pepper in one bowl. Place the bread crumbs in the second. Cut the chicken cutlets in half so they will neatly fit inside the biscuits (you don't want them too big or too small). Dip each cutlet in the egg, then completely coat it in bread crumbs. Coat a baking sheet with the cooking spray and lay the cutlets on it. Also coat the cutlets well.
5. Bake the cutlets for 10 minutes, flip them over, coat the other side with the cooking spray, and bake until golden brown and cooked through, 10 to 12 minutes more.
6. Spoon 1 tablespoon of warm marinara sauce over each cutlet and top it with a slice of mozzarella. Stick the cutlets back in the oven for a couple minutes to melt the cheese.
7. Slice the garlic biscuits open and paint the inside top and bottom with some warm marinara. Place a piece of chicken on each bottom biscuit, pop on the top, and enjoy!

BUFFALO CHICKEN CALZONE

When our daughter Mary returned from Boston College, she'd turned into a lover of all things Buffalo. Suddenly there was less room in the refrigerator, because she'd have Kathy buy all the Frank's RedHot sauce flavors—and there were a lot. And yes, just like Hillary Clinton, Mary would keep a travel-size hot sauce in her handbag . . . just in case Panera Bread didn't have Frank's RedHot *Xtra Hot* sauce on the table.

We started making this calzone because all the kids love pizza, the cream cheese is divine when melted, and this version is Buffalo-saucy enough to keep Mary eating at home. By the way, I read this on Thrillist about Buffalo sauce, "Capsaicin (which is what makes peppers hot) has antioxidant, anti-inflammatory, and anticancer properties. But it's most effective when combined with fats, which means Buffalo wings are basically a health food. You're welcome."

So thank you, Mary, for introducing us to hot sauce and perhaps adding years to our lives, which offsets the year you took off our lives when you learned how to drive. That you could be both a center-line crosser and a mailbox hugger shows just how early you were able to multitask.

2 cups diced or shredded cooked chicken breast
¼ cup hot Buffalo sauce (we use Frank's, as you know)
¾ cup crumbled blue cheese
4 ounces cream cheese, cut into cubes, at room temperature

¼ cup chopped green onions (green tops only)
3 slices bacon, cooked and crumbled
15-ounce store-bought pizza dough, at room temperature
Egg wash: 1 egg whisked with 1 tablespoon water

1. Preheat the oven to 375°F convection (or 350°F standard). Line a baking sheet with parchment paper.

2. In a medium bowl, combine the chicken, hot sauce, blue cheese, cream cheese, green onions, and bacon and mix well (the cream cheese is challenging to blend).

3. Roll the pizza dough into a round 16 inches in diameter and set it on the baking sheet.

4. Imagine a line across the center of the pizza dough (like an equator). Place the chicken/sauce/cheese mixture on one side of the equator, leaving at least ½ inch uncovered at the edges. Fold the dough over itself, lining up the edges. Use a fork to crimp the edges like a pie crust. Stab a couple vent holes on top and brush the whole surface with the egg wash.

5. Bake until the calzone is perfectly golden (and looking like something Bobby Flay would pull from his oven with 15 seconds left on the clock), 18 to 22 minutes, turning once midway. Let rest at least 5 minutes, as the filling will be very hot before serving.

EVERYDAY ENTRÉES

OUR BEST MEALS TODAY ARE SIMPLE, everyday meals at home.

Peter announced he was coming home for a few days and asked if he could invite a new friend of his from Washington. Of course—any friend of Peter's is a friend of ours. Kathy asked what the friend liked, and Peter was very specific: "Steaks. Johnny Walker Blue Label, Grey Goose, Cabernet, and Coors Light." Hmmm, four kinds of booze and only one food item? I forgot to mention, Peter's friend was a Navy SEAL.

The day of their arrival I was cleaning up the kitchen and saw that Kathy had bought all four *liquors*, made her basil pasta *and* fancy appetizers, *and* had baked desserts all afternoon.

"You made him cookies *and* a cake?" I inquired.

She said nothing as she unpacked those really big shrimp from the store where Peter worked as a kid that were nearly forty bucks a pound.

"Wait . . . shrimp *and* steak? Isn't that a little overkill?"

"He's an *American hero*," she said in a voice that sounded a little irritated.

"Yeah, but don't you think you're going a little overboard for this guy?"

And then she responded, epically, "He killed bin Laden!"

Years before anybody knew the name of the Navy SEAL who killed bin Laden, Peter crossed trails with Rob O'Neill, who was indeed an American hero.

"I know, but Blue Label *and* Grey Goose *and* Cabernet?"

"He shot bin Laden!" she said, glaring at me with that look that at Husband School they teach you to avoid at all cost.

Family barbecuing since 1986.

Okay, he had killed bin Laden, and now he was killing our food budget.

Add this to the equation: Because of what he'd done, Rob was wanted by Al-Qaeda, who had put a bounty on his head and had announced he was their number one worldwide target, which meant we couldn't mention to anybody that *he* was staying in the spare bedroom, or we'd have to worry about a truck bomb during the dessert course.

I'm pretty frugal (and still have my First Holy Communion money), and the sheer volume of food and booze was shocking. There was no way we could eat and drink all of that stuff, and wasting *anything* bothers me. But I wasn't counting on Rob picking up his cell phone and inviting half a dozen friends to drop by our house at 10:30 that night—whatever leftovers we had were inhaled. I left the party for bed around 11:30, and according to sources on the ground, dancing broke out in the kitchen at approximately zero dark thirty.

The American hero had apparently been dancing with Mrs. Doocy and twirled her for the first time since she'd had total knee replacement, and that sudden snap in her knee meant it was time for an Advil and bed.

The next morning, every food item was gone as well as all of the hooch. Peter was moving slowly, but Rob bounced down the stairs and asked what was for breakfast. We marveled at his liver function. Brunch was at a fancy buffet, because as you know, *he killed bin Laden,* and we had to show him

Kid Rock golfing with our Kid Peter.

a nation's appreciation. Man, he could drink like a sailor, mainly because he was a sailor.

We actually introduced Rob to a friend we thought he'd get along with, and he did. We know him as Bob Ritchie, but the world knows and loves him as Kid Rock.

One night before Easter, we'd invited Bobby over, even though our brand-new range would not heat above 275°F, so Kathy went to HoneyBaked Ham and bought some emergency side dishes we could warm up in the microwave, *if* her homemade scalloped potatoes and green bean casserole never got cooked. At one point we decided to try them on the Weber grill, and that worked fine. During that extra-long wait, luckily we had a refrigerator in the garage filled with Coors Light to keep the rock star engaged in conversation with our children, who hung on every word until the potatoes were almost bubbling and golden brownish.

It was a wonderful night, and as a welcome-to-the-neighborhood gift, Kid Rock gave us a toilet. Yes, a toilet. Why? It's a long story, but what did you expect from Kid Rock—a Keurig?

An epic storyteller, great entertainer, and shockingly straight talker, Bobby later told Peter, "Your mom is the best cook. She knows exactly what people like to eat."

We can all learn a lesson from Kid Rock. After somebody does something nice for you, pay them a compliment, especially if they've spent the last couple hours making your dinner.

I have always had nice things to say about whatever meal was prepared for me, although there was one time that I was painfully honest with Kathy about a lousy meal, and it still haunts me.

After a good friend's life was saved by a colonoscopy, I made an appointment for one. It was the first time I'd ever been medically sedated. They knocked me out, did their business, and then woke me up half an hour later. Semiconscious, I could understand the doctor telling me I was fine. But then he added that the colonoscopy wasn't nearly as challenging as the grilling I got from Mrs. Doocy.

"*Whhhhaaadd?* She was in there, too?" (Note to self: Never ask a gastroenterologist who else was "in there.")

Apparently when I was first wheeled back into the recovery room, I was still deeply sedated and was speaking something that sounded Swedish. Kathy realized that for the first time in our marriage I was in a vulnerable state, with zero filter, and if asked a question I would positively tell her the true truth.

She had to move fast. She asked me two questions. The second was whether I'd ever had an affair.

Kathy later told me I turned toward her and locked one eye with hers (as the other was rolling around in the back of my head) and I said, "Nope, never. I love *youuuuuu*," then I gurgled a little and fell back to sleep.

Her first question was brilliant. She used the technique professional investigators employ during lie detector tests and asked me a control question, something she knew the answer to, to test my honesty.

"Did you like that pesto I made two nights ago?"

With all impulse control gone, I was brutally honest. "You left out the pine nuts . . . it tasted like crap."

And with that, Kathy knew I was telling the truth.

The nurse who'd for years seen similar spousal cross-examinations said it was the first time she'd heard "pine nuts" in the colonoscopy suite. Kathy has always been a trailblazer.

ENGAGEMENT LASAGNA

When Prince Harry popped the question, he and Meghan Markle were roasting a chicken. Apparently the fastest way to a royal's heart is through his stomach with an Ina Garten recipe.

Here in America, Engagement Chicken is *a thing*. It supposedly started over thirty years ago when an editor at *Glamour* magazine gave her assistant a recipe for lemony chicken. She made it for her guy, and he promptly proposed. Three others in the office made it and got engaged. The magazine ran the recipe in a 2003 issue, and it was dubbed Engagement Chicken.

Hundreds have since said it worked for them. But for us it was love at first bite of . . . lasagna.

This is what Kathy made on our *first* date at her house, the same night I told her, "You're going to think I'm crazy, but we're going to get married one day," to which she answered, "You really need to leave."

We were engaged five weeks later. That was more than thirty-two years ago. That's a lot of red sauce under the bridge.

4 tablespoons extra-virgin olive oil
1 large yellow onion, cut into medium dice
6 garlic cloves, minced
1 pound sweet Italian sausage, casings removed
1 pound ground sirloin
One 28-ounce can crushed tomatoes (San Marzano is our favorite)
Half a 6-ounce can tomato paste
¾ cup red wine

6 basil leaves
1 tablespoon sugar
1 tablespoon Italian seasoning
½ teaspoon freshly grated nutmeg
¼ teaspoon freshly ground black pepper
1 teaspoon salt
One 16-ounce container ricotta cheese
¼ cup grated Parmesan cheese
3 tablespoons chopped fresh flat-leaf parsley
2½ cups shredded mozzarella cheese
9 lasagna noodles, cooked
Cooking spray

1. In a large skillet, heat 2 tablespoons of the olive oil over medium-high heat. Add the onion and one-third of the chopped garlic and sauté until the onion is translucent, about 5 minutes. Use a slotted spoon to transfer the mixture to a large stockpot.

2. Back in the skillet, cook the Italian sausage until browned thoroughly, breaking it into crumbles as you go. Transfer it to the stockpot.

3. Add the remaining 2 tablespoons olive oil, half the remaining garlic, and the ground sirloin and cook until browned, stirring often. Transfer it to the stockpot.

4. To the stockpot, add the remaining minced garlic, tomatoes, tomato paste, wine, basil, sugar, Italian seasoning, nutmeg, black pepper, and ½ teaspoon of the salt. Bring to a boil over medium heat, then reduce the heat to a simmer and cook for 30 minutes, stirring occasionally.

5. Preheat the oven to 350°F.

6. In a medium bowl, combine the ricotta, Parmesan, parsley, ½ cup of the mozzarella, and the remaining ½ teaspoon salt. Add one-quarter of the meat sauce and stir until smoothly blended.

7. Spread ¼ cup of the red sauce evenly in a 9 x 13-inch baking dish. Lay in an even layer of 3 noodles (try not to overlap). Spread on one-third of the remaining sauce, then half the ricotta cheese mixture. Add another layer of 3 noodles, followed by one-third of the remaining sauce, then the remaining cheese mixture. Top with a final layer of 3 noodles and the remaining sauce. Top evenly with the remaining mozzarella.

8. Coat a large piece of foil with cooking spray and lay it oil side down over the lasagna. Bake until bubbling, about 45 minutes. Remove the foil and bake 10 minutes more. Let stand for 15 minutes before serving.

KID ROCK'S MOM'S CHICKEN POT PIE

Kid Rock loves his beer cold, his cars fast, and his mama's cooking on the table. I was talking with him and his mother, Susan Ritchie, and asked him what she prepares that makes him happy. He casually turned to her and asked, "Mom, what are those little things with the stuff you make in the oven?"

"Pot pies."

"*Yes!* That's the thing with the stuff in the oven!"

Susan's recipe is clever—it uses puff pastry shells instead of pie dough. And it makes a lot, so it's perfect if it's 3 a.m. and you've just invited the band over to your mom's house.

"It's a whole meal in a little pie," Bob says. And he's right.

Two 10-ounce packages Pepperidge Farm Puff Pastry Shells
2 cups diced (½-inch) carrots
1½ cups diced (½-inch) celery
¾ teaspoon kosher salt
1¼ cups diced (½-inch) onion
¾ cup frozen peas
9 tablespoons butter
¾ cup + 2 tablespoons flour
½ teaspoon ground white pepper
¼ cup + 2 tablespoons Better Than Bouillon chicken base
4 cups diced or shredded rotisserie chicken
Milk (optional)

1. Preheat the oven to 425°F.

2. Set the pastry shells on a baking sheet and bake them according to the package directions. Set aside to cool, then remove the tops.

3. Meanwhile, in a medium saucepan, combine the carrots, celery, salt, and 1½ cups water. Bring to a boil over medium-high heat and cook until just tender, about 5 minutes. Add the onion and boil 5 more minutes. Add the peas to warm them through. Drain the vegetables and run them under cold water to stop the cooking. Set aside.

4. In a Dutch oven, melt the butter over low heat. Whisk in the flour and white pepper and cook, whisking constantly, until the mixture has thickened, about 1 minute. Stir 3 cups water into the chicken base, then add to the pot and cook, stirring, until thick.

5. Add the vegetables and chicken to the sauce and cook until heated through. If the sauce is too thick, stir in a bit of milk.

6. To serve, divide the chicken mixture among the pastry shells and top with the pastry lids. Spoon additional chicken mixture on top if desired, and some around the base. (If you still have leftover chicken mixture, serve it the next day over mashed potatoes.)

DENTAL HYGIENIST'S POT ROAST

Kathy and I have dozens of pot roast recipes, but for this cookbook we've narrowed down our favorites to my mom's and this one. They are both very retro, with the flavor coming from a couple of cans of soup mixed in. But it's the can of *cranberries* that makes this special. And also the person who told us about it.

Kathy got this from her dental hygienist during one of her twice-yearly cleanings. You ever notice how many questions chatty technicians ask that you'd like to answer, but they have their tools in your mouth?

"What are you making for dinner?" she inquired from behind her safety mask.

"Aaarrgeg blluh-klah," Kathy gurgled, midcleaning.

"I've got something you've never tried . . ." and she was right.

At the end of the appointment, the hygienist wrote down the basics for this recipe on the back of a graphic gingivitis brochure, which scared us all into brushing three times daily. For a week.

2- to 3-pound boneless beef chuck roast
Salt and freshly ground black pepper
2 tablespoons extra-virgin olive oil
3 garlic cloves, smashed
1 or 2 pinches herbes de Provence
Cooking spray
One 10.5-ounce can cream of chicken soup

One 14-ounce can whole-berry cranberry
    sauce
1 tablespoon flour (optional)
1 tablespoon butter (optional)
Cooked egg noodles or mashed potatoes,
    for serving (dealer's choice)

1. Sprinkle the roast generously with salt and pepper.

2. In a large skillet, heat the olive oil over medium-high heat. Add the garlic and cook 30 seconds, then add the roast and brown it well all over, about 5 minutes on each side. Sprinkle with the herbes de Provence.

3. Coat a slow cooker insert with cooking spray. Pour in the cream of chicken soup, then add the roast. Spoon the cranberry sauce on top.

4. Cover the slow cooker and cook on low for 8 hours, until tender.

5. Carve the meat, place the roast on a serving plate (leave the liquid in the cooker), and cover it with foil.

6. Half of our family likes to top it with a little gravy. To make that, give the liquid in the cooker a stir, add the flour and butter, and stir until melted.

7. Serve the gravy over the roast on top of egg noodles or mashed potatoes.

8. In honor of the source of this recipe, please floss immediately following the meal.

ROCKET CHICKEN

On our first family trip to Europe we discovered something new: an exotic lettuce-y plant we'd never ever had before called arugula, which is referred to as rocket over there. A waiter told us that arugula salad could fight cancer and was a natural aphrodisiac. He said, smirking, "I've got six kids, and I blame the arugula!"

I've heard "blame it on the alcohol" before, but blaming it on the salad was a new one.

As the kids whispered, "What's an aphrodisiac?" we made a note, and when we returned home we started experimenting with arugula . . . for the health benefits, not the other one.

This recipe is an adaptation of two favorite "salad on chicken" dishes, Milanese and chicken capricciosa, which is a specialty at a local place called Aldo's in northern New Jersey that has been making us happy for over twenty years.

**3 tomatoes, seeded and cut into ½-inch
  chunks
¼ cup diced (½-inch) red onion
1 large garlic clove, minced
¾ cup extra-virgin olive oil, plus more as
  needed
Salt and freshly ground black pepper
2 large eggs
1 cup plain dried bread crumbs
6 thin-sliced chicken breast cutlets
4 cups baby arugula
Freshly grated Parmesan cheese**

1. In a medium bowl, combine the tomatoes, onion, garlic, ¼ cup of the olive oil, and salt and pepper to taste. Give a good stir and refrigerate for 1 hour before you start the chicken.

2. In two shallow bowls, make a breading assembly line. Whisk the eggs in one bowl and combine the bread crumbs and salt and pepper to taste in the second. Drag each cutlet through the egg mix and then coat it with the bread crumbs. Repeat to bread all the chicken and set aside.

3. In a large skillet, heat the remaining ½ cup olive oil over medium-high heat. Working in batches and adding more oil as needed, fry the cutlets until golden brown, flip, and fry the other side until cooked through. Set aside on paper towels to soak up any extra oil.

4. To serve, place a cutlet on a plate and top with a mound of arugula. Top with a tablespoon or two of the tomato-onion mixture and a sprinkle of Parmesan. Last, drizzle with some of the liquid from the tomato bowl.

5. The rocket is ready for liftoff. Houston, we have an entrée. . . .

Pictured with Jersey
Corn Ravioli (page 84)

BACON-WRAPPED MEAT LOAVES

• MAKES 8 SERVINGS •

When my mom would holler from the kitchen, "Stephen, can you come here and crush your mother some Ritz crackers," I knew it was meat loaf night. Served with a can of sweet peas and her creamy mashed potatoes with a melting pat of butter on top, that was living.

This is my mom's recipe, updated with the sensibilities of this millennium. You know, wrapped in bacon.

1 tablespoon butter
1 cup medium-diced yellow onion
2 garlic cloves, minced
2 pounds lean ground beef
1 tablespoon Worcestershire sauce
2 large eggs, lightly whisked
½ cup crushed Ritz crackers (about 12)
1 teaspoon salt
1 teaspoon freshly ground black pepper
8 slices thick-cut bacon
½ cup ketchup
2 tablespoons packed light brown sugar
1 teaspoon smoked paprika
French's French-Fried Onions, for garnish
   (optional)

1. Preheat the oven to 350°F.

2. In a medium skillet, melt the butter over medium heat. Add the onion and sauté until softened, 3 or 4 minutes. Add the garlic and sauté until fragrant, 1 or 2 minutes more, then let it cool down a bit before the next step.

3. In a large bowl, combine the onion/garlic mixture, beef, Worcestershire, eggs, crackers, salt, and pepper. Mixing with bare hands gives you the best result; that's the way my mom did it and it was a thing of beauty.

4. Divide the mixture into 8 equal parts and form them into balls, then flatten them so they look like hamburger hockey pucks.

5. Wrap a slice of bacon around the perimeter of each of the mini meat loaves and place them on a baking sheet.

6. Bake for 50 minutes.

7. Meanwhile, in a small bowl, mix together the ketchup, brown sugar, and smoked paprika.

8. Remove the meat loaves from the oven and spoon about 1 tablespoon of the ketchup glaze over each meat loaf. If you like, sprinkle some French's fried onions on top as well. Bake until the meat is no longer pink and the center has an internal temperature of 165°F, 20 to 25 minutes. Serve.

SEARED SALMON ON AVOCADO CREMA

•MAKES 4 SERVINGS•

When Kathy heard a successful mother being interviewed on the radio say she got all of her kids into Ivy League schools by feeding them fish at breakfast, she had to try that on our kids, to give them a competitive edge, and she did, for two days. By the third day the Doocy kids were begging for Eggos and said that if eating fish for breakfast was how you got into college, they didn't want to go.

Too bad that didn't work, I often think of all the money we could have saved on SAT tutors if Kathy's breakfast-fish experiment had worked. . . .

The funny thing is, now we all eat a lot of salmon, which can get too routine, so we switched it up a few years ago by serving the salmon on top of a mound of Kathy's guacamole. Wow, was that great! Then she had an even better idea—we could swap in the avocado crema that she makes as a sauce for her Tex-Mex dishes, and as it turns out, it's zesty and scrumptious on salmon.

It's that kind of out-of-the-box thinking that could get Kathy into the Ivy League, or at least *Coastal Living.*

1 large avocado, halved and pitted
⅓ cup plain Greek yogurt
2 tablespoons fresh lime juice
⅓ cup fresh cilantro leaves, plus sprigs for garnish
Salt
Four 6-ounce salmon fillets, skin removed
Freshly ground black pepper

1. With a spoon, scoop the avocado into a food processor. Add the yogurt, lime juice, cilantro, and ½ teaspoon salt. Blend until the mixture is very smooth and the cilantro is in tiny specks. Set aside.

2. Dry the salmon fillets between paper towels, then pat lightly with salt and pepper on all sides.

3. Set a nonstick skillet over medium-high heat. When the pan is hot, add the salmon and sear until there is a golden crust on it, 5 to 7 minutes. Carefully flip and sear the other side for 5 to 7 minutes, until done to your liking.

4. Make a small mound or swirl of the avocado crema on a plate and set a piece of salmon on top. Add cilantro sprigs for garnish and serve.

Pictured with Green Beans
and Goat Cheese (page 79)

SPECIAL-EVENT CHILI

The Super Bowl, the Oscars, New Year's Eve, election night—when there's a big, special event on TV, Kathy makes this chili. Early in our marriage we'd invite a bunch of people over, but because we didn't have a proper dining room table or chairs, everybody would get a bowl and find a seat, often on the floor, and settle in to watch TV.

She'd make a batch at Halloween, and when our friends would bring their kids by the house, we'd invite them in for a bowl of chili and maybe an adult beverage while their kids evaluated the treats they'd received and wondered what possessed that family down the street to hand out popcorn balls.

This is the ultimate stick-to-your-ribs bowl of warmth for a cold night.

4 tablespoons extra-virgin olive oil
2 pounds lean ground sirloin
4 garlic cloves, minced
2 medium red onions, chopped
6 celery stalks, cut into medium dice
Two 28-ounce cans crushed tomatoes (we use San Marzano)
4 to 6 tablespoons chili powder, to taste
4 teaspoons kosher salt
2 teaspoons sugar
2 teaspoons Worcestershire sauce

Two 15-ounce cans red kidney beans, drained and rinsed (optional)
Optional toppings: sour cream, guacamole, shredded cheese, chopped green onions, and/or Fritos

1. In a large Dutch oven, heat 2 tablespoons of the olive oil over medium heat. Add the sirloin, breaking it up with a spatula, and cook until browned. Transfer the meat to a plate and set aside.

2. Add the remaining 2 tablespoons olive oil to the pan. Add the garlic and sauté until fragrant, about 30 seconds. Add the onions and celery and cook, stirring, until softened, 5 to 8 minutes.

3. Return the meat to the pot and add the tomatoes, chili powder, salt, sugar, Worcestershire, and beans (if you're a bean person).

4. Preheat the oven to 350°F.

5. Increase the heat to medium-high and bring the chili to a boil. Cover, transfer to the oven, and bake, stirring occasionally, for 2 hours, which thickens and melds the flavors so nicely.

6. Serve with sour cream, guacamole, cheese, green onions, and Fritos (a taste of our childhood).

MISS AUDREY'S VENISON CHILI

When I asked Bob Ritchie, aka Kid Rock, about the foods that make him happy, he mentioned his mom's chicken pot pie (see page 114) and "Audrey's venison chili."

Audrey is Audrey Berry, his fiancée. Both love being in the great outdoors, and often she goes hunting with him at his properties in Tennessee and Alabama. Bob says he's a better shot with a gun, but Audrey is a better bow hunter.

Not only is Audrey a great shot, but she also cleans what they bag and then often cooks it up that same day. Audrey Instagrammed a beautiful elk filet and wrote, "*Best* there is #elk."

So what makes this chili one of his happiest foods? Bob said, "It tastes great and it's free." I think he likes it because it reminds him of Miss Audrey.

CHILI
2 pounds ground venison
2 medium yellow onions, chopped
4 garlic cloves, minced
2 tablespoons unsalted butter
1 tablespoon extra-virgin olive oil
One 28-ounce can diced tomatoes (and their juices)
One 15-ounce can tomato sauce
One 6-ounce can tomato paste
One 16-ounce can light red kidney beans, drained and rinsed
One 16-ounce can dark red kidney beans, drained and rinsed
One 16-ounce can pinto beans or Great Northern beans, drained and rinsed

SEASONINGS
3 tablespoons ground cumin
2 tablespoons chili powder
1 tablespoon Montreal Steak seasoning
1 teaspoon dried oregano
1 teaspoon paprika
½ teaspoon cayenne pepper
Salt and freshly ground black pepper, to taste

TOPPINGS AND ACCOMPANIMENTS (USE ONE OR USE ALL!)
Sour cream
Shredded sharp Cheddar cheese
Chopped white onion
Diced avocado
Fresh cilantro
Cornbread

1. To make the chili: In a large stockpot, combine the venison, onions, garlic, butter, and olive oil. Cook over medium heat, stirring often, until the meat is browned.

2. Add the diced tomatoes, tomato sauce, tomato paste, beans, all the seasonings, and 1½ cups water. Stir to combine and bring to a boil over medium-high heat. Reduce the heat to low and simmer, uncovered and stirring occasionally, until it's thickened, about 1 hour.

3. Serve with your desired toppings and cornbread!

GOLDIE'S CHICKEN

·MAKES 8 SERVINGS·

Our next-door neighbor Goldie was listening to the radio one day when the personal chef for a real-life head of state was asked by the host, "What's the king's favorite meal?" This not being the kind of royal insight you normally get living next to the boring Doocy house, she grabbed a pencil and pad and wrote down this recipe.

The most lovable neighbor a family could have, Goldie remembered everybody's birthdays and graduations, and even though we don't celebrate the same holidays, she always had Christmas cards and presents for the kids.

Goldie is a peaceful person. She once called in a panic because a large winged bug was terrorizing her and asked me to come over, which I did. She instructed me emphatically, *"Steve, don't kill it,"* which made me feel foolish, as I was holding a rolled-up newspaper. "It's a life," she said. So I captured the bug and released it to the outdoors.

Goldie serves this recipe often at her many parties and everybody asks how to make it. They're shocked at how easy it is. When she makes it, Goldie cuts a whole chicken into 8 pieces, but that's too ambitious for us, so we use chicken breast halves and cut them into cutlets.

To this day she does not remember the name of the king who loved this dish, nor the radio station she heard it on. For all we know, the recipe is a favorite of Larry King. And that's why we simply call it Goldie's Chicken. Now that we've shared it with you, you're officially part of our neighborhood, which is good, because next time Goldie calls, you can go and deal with the praying mantis.

4 large boneless, skinless chicken breasts
⅓ cup lower-sodium soy sauce
⅓ cup honey
⅓ cup white wine
Cooking spray

1. Set a chicken breast on a cutting board, lay your hand across the top, and from the fatter side, carefully slice it horizontally into 2 thin, even pieces, creating 2 cutlets. Repeat with the other chicken breasts to make a total of 8 cutlets.

2. In a large bowl, whisk together the soy sauce, honey, and wine. Place the cutlets in the bowl, make sure they're coated in marinade, cover with plastic, and refrigerate for 4 to 6 hours, or overnight if you've planned ahead, turning them in the marinade every couple hours.

3. Preheat the oven to 350°F. Coat a 9 x 13-inch baking dish with cooking spray.

4. Lay the chicken in a single layer in the dish. Cover with foil and bake for 25 minutes. Remove the foil, flip the cutlets, and increase the oven temperature to 400°F. Bake until done, 15 to 20 minutes longer. Once ready, it's time to serve your royal family.

NOTE: *Although this recipe is simplicity itself, it requires a fair amount of marinating time, so plan ahead!*

EASY LEMON CHICKEN

During Peter's junior and senior years of high school, when we took him to different parts of America to look at colleges, we discovered that he and his parents were looking at different aspects of college life.

At one school we asked the admissions staff about the acceptance rate for out-of-state students, but Peter inquired, "What is there to do after class?" We wondered where the closest level-one trauma center was, and he wanted to know how far it was to the closest Applebee's.

On the edge of the University of Virginia campus, Kathy and the kids stayed at a Best Western, where Peter realized that within a few blocks' radius there was a Burger King, Wendy's, Taco Bell, Chili's, and a bunch of pizza joints.

"I could be very happy here . . ." he said with a smile.

Why had we paid a physics tutor $75 an hour to improve his grades to get him into a good college when all he really wanted was 24/7 access to fast food?

When he moved to go to Villanova, we gave him a few family recipes (including this one) to make if he ever had to cook for himself. He did not, because he was within walking distance of Campus Corner, McDonald's, Wingers, Taco Bell, Qdoba, and Five Guys. I'm just learning now that most of them coincidentally sold beer.

Hmmmm.

We love this lemon chicken recipe. I've been making it since I judged a cooking contest in Kansas where this was the winning entrée. As I recall, the person who made it won a waterbed. Go figure.

¾ cup flour
Salt and freshly ground black pepper
⅛ teaspoon garlic powder
4 thin-sliced chicken breasts
3 tablespoons extra-virgin olive oil
¼ cup chicken stock
1 lemon, cut into ¼-inch-thick slices
4 tablespoons (½ stick) butter
1 shallot, finely chopped
¼ cup fresh lemon juice
Minced chives, for garnish

1. Place the flour on a plate. In a small bowl, combine 1 teaspoon salt, ½ teaspoon pepper, and the garlic powder. Sprinkle the mixture lightly on both sides of the 4 cutlets. Dredge the cutlets in the flour, coating them well.

2. In a large skillet, heat the olive oil over medium-high heat. Add the chicken and cook undisturbed for 5 minutes, then flip and cook until golden, no longer pink inside, and cooked through, about 5 minutes. Set the chicken aside on a plate.

3. Add the stock and lemon slices to the pan, reduce the heat to medium, and scrape up the crunchy browned bits of chicken. Add the butter and shallot and sauté for 1 minute, then stir in the lemon juice and cook for about 2 minutes. Season with salt and pepper to taste.

4. To serve, place a cutlet on a plate, drizzle with the lemon sauce, and add a cooked lemon slice on top. Chives add a little color to this tasty dish.

MARTHA MacCALLUM'S ALL-DAY STEW

·MAKES 8 TO 10 SERVINGS·

At the end of a nice restaurant dinner, after splitting a bottle of wine and loudly discussing the day's events and gossiping about our neighbors, we got up to leave and the total strangers who'd been sitting next to us the whole time said, "Hi, Steve, we're Martha MacCallum's parents!"

Surprised to meet them, we immediately rewound what we'd just said over the course of our meal, hoping we'd not spoken anything bad about our neighbor Martha MacCallum. But who could? She's one of the nicest women and greatest mothers we've ever met.

Martha says when she and her husband, Dan, got married, they'd walk into her mom and dad's house on a Sunday and smell this all-day stew cooking and just smile, knowing this was going to be a great dinner. She serves this easy meal with a green salad and French bread and says it makes the whole house smell "football game/November cozy."

Now Martha makes it for her three college kids. As soon as they open the door and smell the stew that's been cooking all day, they know they're home.

3 pounds beef stew meat, cut into 1-inch chunks
½ cup flour
4 teaspoons salt
One 10-ounce can condensed beef broth
2 cups dry Burgundy wine, such as Cabernet or whatever you've got left over
4 carrots, cut into 1-inch chunks
4 russet potatoes, peeled and cut into 1-inch chunks
One 20-ounce bag frozen cut beans (5 cups)
1½ pounds frozen pearl onions (about 18), thawed
1 tablespoon packed light brown sugar
1 bay leaf

1. Preheat the oven to 250°F.
2. In a Dutch oven, toss the meat, flour, and salt until the meat is well coated. Stir in the broth and remaining ingredients, cover, and bake, stirring occasionally, until the meat and vegetables are tender, 5 to 6 hours.

GRANDMA JOANNE'S POT ROAST

This recipe is where we got the idea for this cookbook. My mom first served it when I was probably seven or eight, and I couldn't fathom how any other meal, anywhere on the earth, could be better than this. It has so many memories for me that I can't help but be happy when it's served.

For the last thirty years, Kathy has made this pot roast in the slow cooker on my birthday and when I walk in the house after it has been cooking all day, the aroma takes me back to that little house on Margaret Street in Russell, Kansas, when life was simple, my parents were alive, we were all together, and we had our whole lives ahead of us.

I don't know one person who's eaten this recipe who doesn't love it.

4- to 5-pound trimmed pot roast (chuck, rump, bottom round—all good)
Salt and freshly ground black pepper
¼ cup + 1 tablespoon flour
2 tablespoons vegetable oil
1 yellow onion, peeled, trimmed, and halved
6 carrots, cut into 2- to 3-inch chunks
2 whole celery stalks, ends trimmed, halved
1 pound Yukon Gold potatoes, peeled and quartered
Two 10-ounce cans cream of mushroom soup
1 packet Lipton Onion Soup mix

1. Season the roast generously with salt and pepper and dust it with the ¼ cup flour. Heat a large skillet over medium-high heat, warm the oil, and immediately add the roast. Brown it on all sides, about 5 minutes per side. Transfer the roast to a slow cooker.

2. Back in the hot skillet, add the onion, carrots, celery, and potatoes and cook until lightly browned, about 5 minutes. Add them to the cooker, nestling them around the beef.

3. In a large bowl, combine the soup and Lipton soup packet. Fill an empty soup can with water and add it to the mixture. Mix well and pour over the roast.

4. Cover the slow cooker and cook on low for 8 to 10 hours, until it's fall-off-the-bone tender. (Cramped for time, we've done it on high in 4 hours, and it turns out terrific.)

5. Remove the roast and vegetables to a serving platter and cover with foil to keep warm.

6. Pour the cooking juices into a medium saucepan and bring to a boil over medium heat. Cook, stirring often, up to 10 minutes or until nice and thick.

7. Meanwhile, in a small bowl, mix the remaining 1 tablespoon flour with 2 tablespoons cold water. Mix until smooth, then whisk it into the juices in the saucepan. Stir until you have a thickened gravy.

8. Serve the gravy in a gravy boat alongside the pot roast and vegetables as the crowning glory to the world's greatest meat entrée for under five bucks a pound.

GRANDMA'S GOULASH

I did not eat "pasta" until I was thirty years old. That's because where I came from everybody I knew called pasta either "noodles" or "macaroni." I can still hear my mom saying, "Stephen, bring me a box of macaroni," to make this very goulash, which was always a crowd-pleaser.

When I grew up I decided that if I was going to make Grandma's goulash, I was going to add some booze to it, because wine seems to make many things taste a little better. *Pasta, schmasta.* Thanks, Grandma!

I don't remember us ever having leftovers to put in Mom's Tupperware (which she bought at an actual Tupperware party in the neighbor's living room). But I do remember longing for the day when I'd be old enough to go to a Tupperware party with my friends. It sounded so exotic to a six-year-old kid. A party at the neighbor's house, no kids allowed. How did I know it was really just a bunch of home cooks learning how to burp a plastic box?

1 pound lean ground beef
1 yellow onion, chopped
3 garlic cloves, minced
1½ teaspoons salt
½ teaspoon freshly ground black pepper

One 15-ounce can diced tomatoes (and their juices)
One 15-ounce can tomato sauce
1 cup red wine or beef stock
1 tablespoon Worcestershire sauce
2 cups elbow macaroni (about half a 16-ounce package)
2 ounces cream cheese, at room temperature
¾ cup shredded Cheddar cheese
Toasted crusty bread, for serving

1. In a large saucepan, brown the ground beef over medium-high heat, stirring often, until it's about half cooked. Add the onion, garlic, salt, and pepper and sauté until the meat is cooked and the onion is softened, about 10 more minutes. Pour in the tomatoes, tomato sauce, wine, Worcestershire, and 1 cup water. Stir, bring to a simmer, and cook for 10 minutes, until it's almost bubbling.

2. Add the macaroni and cook until tender, about 15 minutes. Do not overcook or the elbows will start falling apart.

3. Just before serving, stir in the cream cheese and mix until melted and blended. Toss in the Cheddar, give a stir, and serve with the toasted bread.

FRENCH BEEF STEW

·MAKES 6 SERVINGS·

In our town, whenever a new baby arrived or a friend was hospitalized, a group of Kathy's mom friends would organize a friendship basket to help the family eat a good home-cooked meal while they were getting back to normal. She would load up a picnic basket with a bottle of wine, a loaf of bread, a green salad, and either this beef stew or the recipe for Bobby's Goulash, which Kathy loved, from a Paula Deen cookbook.

We were trying to remember where we first had this dish, and our best guess is the World Showcase of restaurants at Walt Disney World. They made something like this at Chefs de France, and it was such a wonderful night of fun with the kids that we tried to replicate the taste . . . and it's pretty close.

Actually we're always looking for an excuse to cook with red wine, and a new baby down the block seems like as good a reason as any.

1 tablespoon extra-virgin olive oil
6 garlic cloves, minced
4-pound chuck roast, cut into 1½-inch chunks
Salt and freshly ground black pepper
6 carrots, cut into 1-inch chunks
2 medium yellow onions, roughly chopped
3 cups dry red wine
⅛ teaspoon freshly grated nutmeg

One 28-ounce can crushed tomatoes (we prefer San Marzano)
2 tablespoons tomato paste
2 celery stalks, cut into 1-inch chunks
1 teaspoon fresh rosemary leaves, roughly chopped
1 pound white mushrooms, trimmed and halved
2 cups beef stock
Mashed potatoes, for serving

1. Preheat the oven to 325°F.
2. In a large skillet, heat the olive oil over medium-high heat. Add one-third of the garlic and cook for 30 seconds, then stir and add the beef. Add a pinch each of salt and pepper and brown the meat on all sides, about 5 minutes per side. Transfer the beef to a Dutch oven.
3. Add the carrots and onions to the skillet and sauté until browned and softened, 5 to 8 minutes. Add them to the Dutch oven with the beef.
4. To the Dutch oven, add the wine, remaining garlic, nutmeg, 1 teaspoon salt (or more to taste), and 1 teaspoon pepper and give a good stir. Add the tomatoes and paste, celery, rosemary, mushrooms, and stock. Mix well.
5. Cover and braise in the oven until the meat is tender, about 2½ hours.
6. Serve over mashed potatoes.

MAMA MARIE'S MEATBALLS

•MAKES 12 TO 14 EGG-SIZE MEATBALLS•

Brian Kilmeade's mother is a genius.

When Brian was in college he would drive home to Massapequa, New York, every two weeks because his mother, Marie, promised that if he came home to visit, she'd make him the meatballs he and his brothers grew up loving. It was a great deal for both of them, because every parent wants their college kid to come home to visit, and every college kid wants free food.

After a nice visit home, Marie would load Brian up with a big Tupperware container and send him back to his dorm at C. W. Post, where upon arrival he'd announce, "I've got the meatballs!" The entire hall would run to his room for a taste of home—even if it wasn't *their* home.

This motherly gesture was also super helpful for Brian's tight college budget. He worked hard and received academic and athletic financial aid, but his mom's home-cooked specialty helped stretch those dollars.

But the meatball love didn't end at graduation. When Brian moved to Los Angeles to follow his dreams, his mother would send him off from JFK Airport with a suitcase full of affection. Of course, that couldn't happen today; the TSA would surely have to taste-test a couple and he'd be missing more than a few by the time he got home to Malibu.

Brian's mother is a wonderful person, a great cook, and a loving grandmother who's now enjoying her retirement after a successful career in New York City. Marie told me that recounting this recipe was tough, because she's never written

down a recipe; she's always cooked by feel. You know, she'd taste it and add a little of this and a little of that, and next thing you know, it's perfect. Moms are good at that. Serve these meatballs with your favorite pasta.

SAUCE
3 tablespoons extra-virgin olive oil
1 small onion, thinly sliced
2 garlic cloves, thinly sliced
Two 28-ounce cans crushed tomatoes
One 6-ounce can tomato paste

MEATBALLS
1½ pounds ground sirloin
2 large eggs
1¼ cups Italian-style dried bread crumbs
2 tablespoons dried minced onion
1 tablespoon dried minced garlic
½ teaspoon garlic salt
½ teaspoon freshly ground black pepper
3 tablespoons minced fresh flat-leaf parsley
½ cup grated Pecorino Romano cheese
2 tablespoons extra-virgin olive oil
4 Italian sausage links (2 hot and 2 sweet), cooked
4 basil leaves

1. To make the sauce: In a large saucepan, heat the olive oil over medium-high heat. Add the onion and garlic and sauté until tender, 5 to 8 minutes. Add the tomatoes and paste, give them a good stir, and let simmer as you make the meatballs.

2. To make the meatballs: In a large bowl, combine the meat, eggs, bread crumbs, ¾ cup water, dried onion, dried garlic, salt, pepper,

parsley, and Pecorino Romano and gently
mix until smooth. Roll the mixture into 12 to
14 meatballs, each the size of a large egg.

3. In a large skillet, heat the olive oil over
medium-high heat, swirling to coat the pan. Add
the meatballs and cook until evenly browned on
the outside, gently turning them as needed.

4. Transfer the meatballs to the tomato sauce and
add the sausage links and basil leaves. Make sure
everything is submerged in the sauce and bring
the sauce to a simmer over medium heat. Cover
and cook, occasionally giving a gentle stir, until the
meatballs are cooked through (cut a meatball in
half to be sure), 45 to 50 minutes.

RED PEPPER PASTA

This is a recipe from a neighbor who told us that jarred roasted peppers are lousy: "You have to make your own." So Kathy tried roasting her own one afternoon. I came home and as soon as I opened the door, it smelled like the house was on fire. But the closer I got to the kitchen, the more it smelled like somebody was smoking weed.

The second time she made them, a plumber was supposed to be upstairs installing the washer and dryer, which was a very big job. I arrived home and saw the plumber's van in the driveway, and when I walked into the kitchen I was surprised to see him lounging at our kitchen island with a full cup of coffee as he ate a piece of pie, watching Kathy roast the peppers over the open flame on our Thermador cooktop. It smelled like she was using recreational marijuana in the production of the meal . . . again. But that's what burning peppers smell like. The plumber had a big grin on his face and turned to me and said, "Steve, it takes a *real woman* to roast peppers for her man. . . ."

No doubt about it, I was lucky that Kathy was trying so hard to make it right. Apparently the plumber's wife was not a pepper roaster, and he admired those who are. But more important—

why was I paying him $150 an hour to watch my wife make our house smell like the set of a Cheech and Chong movie?

6 red bell peppers
¾ cup fat-free half-and-half
½ cup store-bought Italian vinaigrette
1 cup fresh basil leaves
Salt and freshly ground black pepper
1 pound fettuccine noodles, cooked
Grated Parmesan cheese, for serving

1. Blacken the bell peppers over the open flame of your stove or on an outdoor grill, turning as each side gets more charred. When no red is left, wash the peppers in cold water so that the skin sheds from them. Cut the peppers into chunks, discarding the seeds and stems, and place in a food processor. Add the half-and-half, vinaigrette, basil, and salt and black pepper to taste and process until smooth.

2. Toss with the cooked fettuccine noodles and sprinkle Parmesan on top. Serve and enjoy. (P.S. Air out the house before your local clergy drops by for tea.)

POTATO CHIP CHICKEN

When Kathy was living in New York doing TV commercials, she was friends with a very funny young bartender who wanted to be an actor. Trying to help the guy get his first big break, Kathy took him to her TV commercial agent, who said he was a nice enough guy, but he simply was not "commercial enough."

Her agent turned down Bruce Willis.

When Bruce was one of the first backers of Planet Hollywood, Kathy would call and he'd put us on a list so we wouldn't be stuck at the velvet rope. All of our kids wound up having birthday parties there, as guests of Mr. Willis, which meant the waiters were extra friendly because they didn't want word getting back to Mr. Die Hard that they weren't fantastic.

Our kids loved Planet Hollywood's famous Cap'n Crunch Chicken, and we tried making it a couple times at home but our version was never as good. So we swapped out the Cap'n for the crunch of potato chips, and this recipe became a happy reminder of a happy time.

6 cups potato chips (Lay's are great)
2 teaspoons garlic powder
½ cup grated Parmesan cheese
¼ teaspoon freshly ground black pepper
4 tablespoons (½ stick) butter, melted

3 boneless, skinless chicken breasts, halved horizontally to make 6 thin cutlets
Cooking spray
Sweet and sour sauce or salsa, for serving (optional)

1. Preheat the oven to 400°F. Line a baking sheet with foil.
2. In a food processor, pulse the potato chips into crumbs. (You can crush them in a plastic bag, too, but the machine makes more even crumbs.)
3. In two shallow bowls, make a breading assembly line. Place the potato chip crumbs in one bowl and mix in the garlic powder, Parmesan, and pepper. Pour the melted butter into the second bowl.
4. Working with one at a time, dip the cutlets first in the butter bowl and then in the crumb mixture, taking care to coat them thoroughly.
5. Place the cutlets on the prepared baking sheet, and if you'd like to push some more of the potato chip coating onto the chicken, be our guest. Give each cutlet a good squirt of cooking spray.
6. Bake until the coating is golden and the chicken is cooked through, usually about 30 minutes.
7. Serve as is, or with sweet and sour sauce or salsa.

GREG NORMAN'S MOM'S CRISPY CRACKLING ROAST PORK

Did you know that Greg Norman, the world-famous golfer and businessman, is a real foodie with a refined palate who also markets fancy Wagyu beef? Greg grew up working cattle in Australia's north and knows something about how to cook up a wonderful meal. On weekends, his mother would roast a big dinner of chicken, lamb, duck, or pork. His mother's specialty was an Australian favorite, crispy crackling roast pork. It's all about the crispy skin. Yes, the Shark loves skin.

Because most American groceries don't sell pork with skin on it, you might have to special-order it. I spoke with our local butcher and he said he could order a pork shoulder with the skin on it, then he also boned and rolled it. As the recipe recommends, the butcher also scored the skin, which helps create the legendary crackling.

This recipe requires a super-hot oven (which made enough smoke to set off our smoke alarm), but the preparation is a snap. The hardest part will be finding the right pork—during my search I told one meat department employee that this was for an Australian recipe, and when I told him the pork *had* to have the skin on it, he stared at me like I was ordering kangaroo. Come on, mate—I go to a different store for that!

3- to 4-pound skin-on boneless pork shoulder, rolled and tied, with the skin scored (ask your butcher)
2 to 3 tablespoons extra-virgin olive oil

3 tablespoons sea salt
5 or 6 large potatoes, quartered, or 20 new potatoes
1 pound baby carrots, or 10 carrots, peeled and cut up
Olive oil cooking spray, for the roasting pan
1 large yellow onion, quartered
Freshly ground black pepper

1. Preheat the oven to 500°F.

2. Rub the pork all over with the oil, making it nice and shiny. Generously sprinkle with the salt. Place in an oven pan skin side up. Roast for 30 minutes to get the skin on the path to Crispy Town. Reduce the oven temperature to 325°F and roast until done. (For crispy perfection, don't brush or baste; you want a dry outside.) For medium doneness, look for 160°F on a meat thermometer inserted into the center of the roast. (Greg's mom says you'll know it's done when you poke it with a skewer and no red juice oozes out.) Cooking times will vary, but a rule of thumb on this is to plan on 25 to 30 minutes per pound, and then in a unique twist to her recipe, Greg's mom will roast it for an extra 25 to 30 minutes.

3. About 1 hour before the pork is done, place the potatoes, carrots, and onion in a greased roasting pan with salt and pepper to your liking. Roast next to the pork for its final hour.

4. Let the meat rest 15 to 20 minutes, then carve away. Serve with the vegetables.

RITZ CRACKER–BREADED PORK CHOP

When I was growing up, Mom always served her late Sunday afternoon appetizers on Ritz crackers. I remember as a five-year-old eating a lot of pickled herring, smoked oysters, and Braunschweiger, stopping the day I was old enough to read the list of ingredients . . . mainly pork liver with additional pork liver. Enough said.

My mom loved Ritz crackers, and we thought she was a pioneer when she had us pulverize a tube of them to use as breading on these pork chops.

My kids love this recipe, but we never told them what it was made of; they just didn't like pork. So thanks to some benign misinformation campaign by the cook, our kids grew up thinking this was some kind of exotic chicken finger.

4 tablespoons (½ stick) butter, cut into small chunks, plus more for the baking dish
3 large eggs
3 cups crushed Ritz crackers (about 72 crackers)
¼ teaspoon freshly ground black pepper
8 boneless center-cut pork chops
Butter-flavored cooking spray

1. Preheat the oven to 400°F. Butter a large baking dish—9 x 13-inch usually works great.
2. In two shallow bowls, make a breading assembly line. Whisk the eggs in one bowl. Stir together the crushed crackers and pepper in the second. Set the baking dish at the end.
3. Dredge a pork chop in the eggs, then coat it in crackers, making sure every inch is covered, which may mean smashing more crackers onto the chop and pressing them in place. Set the chop in the baking dish and repeat with the rest.
4. Coat the chops with cooking spray, then prop the chunks of butter on the sides (this will add wonderful flavor as it melts).
5. Cover the dish with foil and bake for 15 minutes. Remove the foil and bake until the juices run clear and there's no pink inside, another 25 to 30 minutes. A good internal temperature is 145°F, according to the National Pork Board. (Who knew there was a National Pork Board?)
6. Let the chops rest for 5 minutes, then serve.

Pictured with Pesto
Grilled Corn (page 77)

GERT'S CRAB CAKES

During my first book tour, we visited a bookstore in Bryn Mawr, Pennsylvania, just a few miles down the road from Villanova University, where Peter Doocy was studying politics. That was the day an elegant woman and her daughter, who was holding about a dozen books, asked if I could autograph them. Making a dozen sales, I happily signed away as the woman, Eileen Hansen, told me they were big fans of Fox News Channel and watched every day.

She told me her family owned and operated the Normandy Farms Resort Hotel in Blue Bell, Pennsylvania, and next time we had a problem finding a hotel to give them a call. Come the next parents' weekend at Villanova, we indeed had hotel trouble, so we called and started a wonderful friendship that lasted Peter's four years in college; in fact, the Hansen family threw him a graduation party.

Several years later, when Mary was studying law at Villanova, she fell on the ice in the law school parking lot and broke her right arm. No, we didn't sue the law school—that's just asking for trouble. But with her arm shattered, Mary couldn't take notes, so Kathy moved in and started going to class with her as her stenographer. ("I didn't know what was important, so I wrote down everything!")

Her second night as note-taker, a blizzard and ice storm knocked out the electricity to the area, so Kathy called Eileen and they found a room in the sold-out hotel for Kathy and Mary, who encamped there for more than a week.

Because they couldn't travel, they ate all their meals at the hotel, and they got hooked on Gert's Crab Cakes, made from an original recipe by Eileen's mother, Gertrude Mary Mehan. This is a happy meal for us not because it reminds us of the broken arm but because it reminds us how lucky we are to have had great friends like Eileen and her husband, Bud.

You can either fry these crab cakes in a skillet on the stove, or deep-fry them (see Deep-Fried Crab Cakes on page 144), which makes it convenient to also make homemade French fries. And don't forget a side of coleslaw. . . .

BÉCHAMEL SAUCE
4 tablespoons (½ stick) butter
¼ cup flour
¾ cup whole milk

CRAB CAKES
16 ounces fresh jumbo lump crabmeat, any shells carefully picked out
4 tablespoons (½ stick) butter
½ cup finely chopped celery
½ cup finely chopped Vidalia onion
½ cup finely chopped green bell pepper
Pinch of cayenne pepper
1 tablespoon Worcestershire sauce
¼ teaspoon Tabasco sauce
1 teaspoon fresh lemon juice
Pinch of freshly grated nutmeg
Salt and ground white pepper
1½ cups plain dried bread crumbs or fine corn flake crumbs
Good-quality extra-virgin olive oil
Tartar sauce or remoulade, for serving

1. To make the béchamel sauce: In a medium saucepan melt the butter over medium heat. Add the flour and whisk, then slowly pour in the milk. Cook, stirring, until thickened and smooth. Set aside.

2. To make the crab cakes: Pat the crabmeat dry. In a large skillet, melt the butter over low heat. Add the celery, onion, and bell pepper and sauté until softened, about 5 minutes. Set the pan aside to let the mixture cool.

3. Add the cayenne, Worcestershire, Tabasco, lemon juice, and nutmeg. Taste and adjust the flavor with salt and white pepper. Stir the béchamel sauce into the vegetables, then fold in the crabmeat and mix gently to blend.

4. Line a baking sheet with wax paper. Using an ice cream scoop, spoon up the crabmeat mixture and form it into 8 to 10 cakes, each about 1½ inches thick. Place them on the lined baking sheet. Cover with another sheet of wax paper and refrigerate for about 10 minutes.

5. Put the bread crumbs in a small bowl, and roll each crab cake in the crumbs until thoroughly coated. Cover and refrigerate again for up to an hour to firm them up before frying.

6. Turn the oven on to warm.

7. In a large skillet, heat a *thin* layer of the olive oil (you don't want too much oil) over medium-high heat. You will probably have to fry the crab cakes in two batches (depending on your pan size); just make sure the crab cakes are not touching one another. Sauté them until golden brown on one side, 4 to 5 minutes. Carefully flip and cook until heated through and golden brown on the second side, another 4 or 5 minutes. Place in the warm oven until serving.

8. Serve hot with tartar sauce or remoulade.

DEEP-FRIED CRAB CAKES

Make the crab cakes as directed through step 4. Preheat a deep-fryer with the appropriate amount of canola oil (check the fryer's manual). Whisk 3 eggs in a shallow dish. Dredge the crab cakes in egg, then coat them with the bread crumbs. Deep-fry the crab cakes until browned, 3 to 5 minutes. Drain slightly on paper towels, keep warm until dinner in the oven, then serve hot with the tartar sauce or remoulade.

KATHY'S CREAMY CASSEROLE

When Kathy was pregnant with Sally and on bed rest, I was responsible for taking care of everything for everybody—which was fine until I broke my foot falling down stairs. I was on crutches, which meant that I couldn't get groceries unless I had help. Luckily I did. Five-year-old Peter would push the cart and three-year-old Mary would assist in gathering things. Mary was at an adorable but irritating stage in which she'd eat only foods that were pink, so as I hobbled ahead on crutches, Mary would put all things pink in our carriage, such as cantaloupe, vodka sauce, pink lemonade, and Funfetti icing.

Peter, thankfully, was responsible and would put exactly what I told him to into the cart. But one time we got to the cashier and there was a problem.

"Peter, we came for flour. Where's the flour?" He held up a dozen daisies. "I said 'flour,' not 'flower.'" As I spoke I realized they sounded exactly the same. I knew I'd better get off those crutches soon, or we'd all die of starvation by winter.

Despite her moratorium on nonpink foods, even Mary would eat this recipe. We all love it, and she often requests it when she comes home from Washington, because it's a happy creamy reminder of her Technicolor childhood.

4 boneless, skinless chicken breasts
½ tablespoon herbes de Provence
2 tablespoons butter
½ cup diced shallots
One 10.5-ounce can cream of mushroom soup
One 10.5-ounce can cream of chicken soup
1 cup whole milk
Freshly ground black pepper
One 16-ounce package egg noodles, cooked and drained
1 cup shredded sharp Cheddar cheese

1. Preheat the oven to 375°F.
2. Lay the chicken breasts on a baking sheet and sprinkle them with the herbes de Provence. Bake until cooked through, 20 to 30 minutes, depending on the thickness. Cut the chicken into ¾-inch cubes and set aside.
3. In a Dutch oven, melt the butter over medium heat. Add the shallots and sauté until soft, about 5 minutes. Add the soups, milk, and ⅛ to ¼ teaspoon ground pepper, to your taste. Cook, stirring often, until the mixture is hot. Toss in the chicken and noodles and stir to combine. Cover the Dutch oven and bake until hot and creamy, about 30 minutes.
4. Uncover, sprinkle on the Cheddar, and bake until the cheese is bubbling and delicious, about 5 minutes.

WORLD'S BEST STEAK WITH BORDELAISE SAUCE

Because I rise in the morning before 99 percent of the American workforce, my big night out on the town is Friday night, when I can stay up late if I take a big nap during Maury Povich. Our favorite place to go is Café Panache in Ramsey, New Jersey. Because it's my night to cut loose, I order a fancy appetizer *and* their signature steak. It's one of those steaks you daydream about all week.

What is it about that steak that's so special? Turns out I didn't need Wikileaks or the Russians to hack into chef Kevin Kohler's kitchen computer; I just asked and he wrote it down for me. There's a lot of stirring on the reduction sauce, but it's so worth it.

Before you eat it, take a picture, because you're going to be talking about how you made the "world's best steak," and you'll need photographic evidence.

4 tablespoons canola oil
6 shallots, thinly sliced
4 garlic cloves, unpeeled
1 cup balsamic vinegar
1 fresh thyme sprig
1 whole clove
2 cups Burgundy wine
8 tablespoons (1 stick) butter
Four 12-ounce best-quality filet or sirloin
    steaks, 1 inch thick, all fat trimmed
Kosher salt and freshly cracked black
    pepper

1. In a medium saucepan, heat 2 tablespoons of the oil over medium heat. Add the shallots and cook until translucent, about 5 minutes. Add the garlic cloves and sauté until nicely golden, 2 to 3 minutes. Add the vinegar, thyme, and clove and cook, stirring, until the sauce is syrupy, at least 2 minutes. Add the wine and bring it to a boil.

2. With the back of your ladle or cooking spoon, push down hard to extract all the liquid from the shallots, garlic, and clove. Cook until the liquid is reduced to ¼ cup, 20 to 30 minutes. Remove from the heat and strain the reduction through a sieve into a bowl. Return the reduction to the pan, then whisk in the butter over medium heat until melted. Keep the sauce warm off the heat.

3. Rub about 1 teaspoon of the oil onto both sides of each steak and season with plenty of salt and freshly cracked black pepper. In a heavy-duty skillet over very high heat, sear the steaks until you have a nice crust on one side, 4 to 5 minutes. Flip the meat using tongs and reduce the heat to medium-high. (Kevin has a tip on judging doneness; see Note).

4. When the steak is done to your liking, remove it from the heat. Let it rest 10 minutes before slicing.

5. Top with the bordelaise sauce to serve, then immediately Instagram *the world's best steak!*

NOTE: *How can you tell when a steak is done medium-rare? Kevin says to squeeze your thumb and index finger together and pinch the fleshy part between the two. When a steak feels the same way, it's medium-rare. The longer you cook the steak, the firmer it gets. You can also use a meat thermometer (the desired internal temperature for medium-rare is 145°F and the temperature for medium steaks should read 160°F, according to the Cattlemen's Beef Board)—just remember that poking the meat lets the juices run out.*

Pictured with Muffin Pan Potatoes (page 85)

MAJOR DAN'S CHICKEN AND NOODLES

Millions of Americans proudly serve in the US military. Ever wonder what they're thinking of when they're thousands of miles away from home?

Chicken and noodles.

That's what does it for Major Dan Rooney of Owasso, Oklahoma, a USAF fighter pilot with three combat tours in Iraq who is widely known today as the founder of the Folds of Honor charity. Major Dan told me, "I think we all have recipes in our lives that have emotion attached to them, and chicken and noodles has always been my homecoming dish."

Dan's wife, Jacqy, was shown how to make this recipe by his mother, Sandy Rooney; it's been a Sunday staple in the Rooney clan for six generations. Dan says, "One of my favorite things about chicken and noodles is that the process is always a family affair. Everyone gets into the mix, and making the dough and cutting the noodles is almost as fun as eating the final product."

"When you're out on the road, you think about it, then when you're finally home you eat it, and it makes you feel really good. It brings our family together. You can taste the emotion."

When Jacqy's making the noodles, it means Dan's coming back soon, they'll finally be together, and most important, *he's safe.*

How many prayers in quiet moments of reflection do the loved ones say waiting for their men and women to return home after being in harm's way? That's why of all the meals in the Rooney repertoire, this one is sacred. "It's that safe hour, when you get to sit down and eat something that makes you feel good, and the world goes away," he says.

"It's my hope and prayer that by sharing our recipe, it will help families come together and create a new tradition," Dan adds. "Our families represent God's greatest gift in life. May this dish at your dinner table bring you peace, happiness, and a full stomach. God bless America!"

> One 4- to 5-pound stewing hen or roaster chicken
> 3 celery stalks, cut into medium dice
> 1 small yellow or white onion, cut into large chunks
> Salt
> 3 large eggs
> 2 cups flour, or more as deisred, plus flour for rolling out the dough
> 1 tablespoon vegetable oil
> Better Than Bouillon brand chicken base (optional)
> Freshly gound black pepper
> Hot mashed potatoes, for serving
> Freshly grated nutmeg (optional), for garnish

1. Dan's mom wanted you to have two different ways to cook the chicken, either in a large saucepan on the stove or in a pressure cooker (which is faster—but not everybody owns one). Just choose the method you're most comfortable with.

METHOD #1: If using a pressure cooker, it needs to be at least an 8-quart cooker. Place in the cooker the chicken, celery, and onion. Season with ½ tablespoon salt, then fill two-thirds to three-quarters of the way up the cooker with water. Do not overfill. Fully close the pressure cooker and cook until the chicken is cooked through, 30 minutes to 1 hour (consult the instructions for your individual cooker, as pressures and timing can vary). Once done, let the cooker cool down, remove the regulator, and then carefully and slowly release the pressure. Never open the cooker when it contains pressure! If you have any questions about safety, always consult your pressure cooker instructions.

METHOD #2: If you want to use a large saucepan, place the chicken, celery, and onion in the pan and cover with water, but don't overfill. Add ½ tablespoon salt and give a stir. Cover the pot and bring to a boil over high heat, then lower the heat to a slow boil and cook up to 1½ hours, or until done through. (You may need to add some more water along the way.) Dan's mom says one way to tell if it's ready is to poke it with a fork. If the meat easily falls off the bone, it's done!

2. Meanwhile, to make the noodles, crack the eggs into a small bowl. In a food processor, combine the flour, oil, ¾ teaspoon salt, and 1 tablespoon water. Turn on the food processor and slowly pour in the eggs all at once. Process until the mixture forms a ball. The dough should not be wet; if it is, add 1 tablespoon flour, and process until smooth.

3. Form the dough into a ball, wrap the dough in plastic wrap, and let it rest for at least 30 minutes.

4. On a lightly floured surface, dust the top of the dough ball with flour, then gently roll into a rectangle ⅛ to 3/16 inch thick. Set aside and let it dry for about 1 hour 30 minutes.

5. Using a sharp knife, cut the dough into noodles ½ inch wide and no more than 3 inches long. Fluff them up a little to make sure they don't stick together.

6. When the chicken is done, remove from the cooker or pot, leaving the broth. Shred the chicken (discard the skin and bones) and set it aside, covering it to keep warm.

7. Taste the broth in the cooker or pot, then add up to 1 tablespoon Better Than Bouillon chicken base, if desired, and salt and pepper to taste until it's seasoned to your liking.

8. Bring the broth to a boil and sprinkle the noodles into the cooker or pot so they don't stick together, then reduce the temperature to medium-high and cook until the noodles are nice and tender but not mushy, about 5 minutes. The only way to know when they're done is to taste them—a little al dente is perfect.

9. To serve, ladle the noodles with a little broth on top of hot mashed potatoes, then top with the warm shredded chicken. Pour more broth over the top if desired, then sprinkle with nutmeg if you like. Serve immediately.

10. *Welcome home, Dan.*

Photo on pages 150–51.

Major Dan's Chicken and
Noodles (page 148)

HAMBURGER PIE

·MAKES 6 SERVINGS·

When I was a little boy my favorite foods were potatoes and hamburgers, and when my mom started peeling the potatoes for hamburger pie, I could hardly wait the hour until suppertime. This is one of those recipes that's an instant way-back machine, taking me to that little house in Russell, Kansas, sitting with my mom in the kitchen waiting for Dad to come home from work as I try to bribe my sisters with *a dime* to do my chores. A dime . . . my, how times have changed.

In the Midwest this is commonly referred to as hamburger pie, but, as in shepherd's pie, there is no pastry crust. I have no idea why a potato-topped casserole is called a pie. It's one of those things that doesn't make sense . . . like why kamikaze pilots wore crash helmets. Ponder that as you peel the potatoes.

3 tablespoons butter, or more as desired, plus butter for the dish
Salt
2 pounds russet potatoes, peeled and quartered
¼ cup milk, or more as desired
Freshly ground black pepper
1½ pounds lean ground beef
1 yellow onion, cut into medium dice
2 garlic cloves, minced
One 10.75-ounce can condensed tomato soup
One 14.5-ounce can diced tomatoes (with their juice)
One 12-ounce bag frozen peas, thawed in hot water
½ cup shredded Cheddar cheese

1. Preheat the oven to 350°F. Grease a 10 x 14-inch oval casserole (or similar-size dish) with butter.
2. In a large saucepan of salted boiling water, cook the potatoes 15 to 20 minutes or until tender. Drain. Transfer them to a stand mixer and add the butter and milk. Whip until smooth. Season with salt and pepper the way you like your potatoes. Set aside. (If you don't have a stand mixer, just make mashed potatoes the way you prefer.)
3. In a large skillet, cook the ground beef over medium-high heat halfway, stirring as needed, and season with ½ teaspoon pepper. Add the onion and garlic and cook, stirring, until the onion is softened and the meat is cooked through. Drain off the excess fat. Reduce the heat to medium, add the tomato soup, diced tomatoes in juice, and peas and simmer a few more minutes to heat through.
4. Place the meat mixture in the prepared dish and smooth out the top. Spoon the mashed potatoes over the meat mixture, spreading it evenly to cover it all. Sprinkle evenly with the Cheddar and bake until heated through and bubbling up, 30 to 35 minutes.
5. Let stand for 5 minutes before serving.

RED WINE CHICKEN

When our daughter Mary comes home, this is one of her most frequently requested meal choices. It makes the whole house smell like Julia Child dropped by and whipped up something while Kathy and I napped in the great room watching *The Five.*

I like it because it has bacon and wine. Enough said.

6 slices bacon, cut into 1-inch pieces
6 garlic cloves, thinly sliced
1 pound button mushrooms, trimmed and halved
2 large yellow onions, cut into 1-inch chunks
3 boneless, skinless chicken breasts, halved horizontally to make 6 thin cutlets
Salt and freshly ground black pepper
2 large potatoes, peeled and quartered
1 pound baby carrots
2 cups red wine or chicken broth
1 teaspoon herbes de Provence
2 cups chicken broth
⅓ cup flour

1. In a Dutch oven, cook the bacon over medium-high heat until crispy. Remove and set aside on a plate.

2. Add the garlic, mushrooms, and onions to the pan with the bacon fat and sauté until they start to brown on the edges, 8 to 10 minutes. Remove the vegetables to the plate with the bacon.

3. Sprinkle about ½ teaspoon salt and ¼ teaspoon pepper on the chicken, lay it in the pan, and cook until browned nicely on both sides, 12 to 15 minutes total.

4. Return the vegetables and bacon to the pot. Add the potatoes, carrots, wine, ½ teaspoon salt, and the herbes de Provence.

5. In a small bowl, combine the broth and flour and stir until smooth. Pour the mixture into the pot and give it a stir. Bring to a boil. Reduce the heat to a simmer, cover, and cook until the chicken is done and the sauce is thickening, 30 to 35 minutes.

6. Season to taste with salt and pepper and serve.

MIKE HUCKABEE'S PORK BUTT

What does a politician know plenty about? Ah . . . pork!

In reality, former governor/presidential candidate Mike Huckabee loves pork . . . pork butt, that is.

Why does it make him happy? Mike says, "There's great pleasure in slow-cook smoking, as it requires patience and *faith*—faith that it will turn out okay ten to twelve hours after you start cooking. And it's such a simple meat that when flavored right puts a smile on people's faces. I love being able to make people ooh and ahh!"

When we smoked this pork butt the first time, I reported our five-star review to the governor, who confessed that his marinade injection recipe is the secret, and that he'd experimented with it over the years until he came up with this one, which he says "broke the code."

This is a two-day operation, with one day spent preparing the meat and the second day smoking it. Plan accordingly. I'm told by the governor that iced tea helps pass the waiting time on your smoky perfection. Mike serves the pork with his smoked corn on the cob, Creole potato salad, and coleslaw. As he says, "You'll have your family and friends begging for more!"

NOTE: *You'll need a marinade injector syringe, easily found online, and a smoker. Mike uses a Masterbuilt 40-inch electric smoker with apple or mesquite chips.*

INJECTION MARINADE
1 cup apple juice
½ cup soy sauce
2 teaspoons Frank's RedHot sauce
3 teaspoons extra-virgin olive oil
1 teaspoon Cajun seasoning (Mike uses Tony Chachere's)
Couple shakes of garlic powder

PORK
5- to 7-pound bone-in pork butt (shoulder)
French's mustard, for rub
Mike's BBQ Rub (page 157) or a store-bought rub of your choice

Barbecue sauce, for serving (optional)

1. To make the injection marinade: In a medium bowl, combine all the ingredients and give a good stir until nice and smooth.

2. To prepare the pork: Fill an injector with the marinade and inject it all deep inside the pork. Rub the pork with a light coating of French's mustard. Generously rub the outside of the pork with BBQ rub, using as much as you can get to stick.

3. Cover the meat and refrigerate overnight.

4. Ideally, you'll be smoking the meat for 10 to 12 hours, which means you need to *start early*. Mike gets up around the time I'm driving into New York to host *Fox & Friends* and fires up the smoker at 4 a.m. Get the meat out of the fridge first and let it sit to get close to room temperature, then set the smoker to 225°F.

5. Place the pork on the middle rack of the smoker with the fat side up. Cook for 8 to 9 hours, then remove the meat from the smoker, wrap it tightly in foil, and return it to the smoker for 2 to 3 hours, until the internal temperature is near 180°F but not more than 200°F.

6. Remove the meat from the smoker and the foil and let it rest for 15 minutes. Using insulated gloves, remove the bone and pull the pork apart.

7. Taste the pork. You can serve barbecue sauce with it, but this recipe is so good you may not want it!

MIKE'S BBQ RUB

·MAKES ENOUGH FOR 2 PORK BUTTS·

½ cup packed light brown sugar
½ cup Splenda Brown Sugar Blend
   (or another ½ cup brown sugar)
¼ cup freshly ground black pepper
1½ tablespoons garlic powder
3 tablespoons onion powder
¼ cup salt
½ cup sweet paprika
¼ cup Accent flavor enhancer (MSG)

In a medium bowl, combine the rub ingredients.

AINSLEY'S MOM'S CHICKEN DIVAN

"My mom loves to cook," Ainsley Earhardt says of her mother, Dale. "Everything she makes turns out perfectly, and she doesn't have to follow a recipe—she just tastes her food and knows instantly what's missing. She shows her family and every guest her love through food, and she loves doing it—maybe because she knows that once you taste her dishes, you're hooked. The best part of walking through her front door and smelling her creations is knowing you're home. A real Southern casserole, and it makes me happy because it will forever remind me of my mother."

We love Dale's Chicken Divan recipe and bet you will, too.

> **4 large or 6 small bone-in, skin-on chicken breasts**
> **Salt and freshly ground black pepper**
> **2 large broccoli heads, cut into florets**
> **One 10.5-ounce can cream of mushroom soup**
> **One 10.5-ounce can cream of chicken soup**
> **1 cup mayonnaise**
> **One 8-ounce container sour cream**
> **1 cup shredded sharp Cheddar cheese**
> **1 tablespoon fresh lemon juice**
> **Butter, for the pan**
> **¼ cup grated Parmesan cheese**
> **Sweet paprika**
> **Baked Rice (recipe follows), for serving**

1. Preheat the oven to 350°F.

2. Lay the chicken breasts skin side up in a single layer in a baking dish or Dutch oven that's at least 4 inches high. Add 3 inches water to the dish, sprinkle with salt and pepper, cover with foil, and bake until the chicken is cooked through, about 45 minutes. Remove the chicken from the oven to cool slightly, but leave the oven on.

3. Meanwhile, in a microwave-safe bowl, steam the broccoli florets in 2 inches water for 4 minutes.

4. In a medium bowl, combine the soups, mayo, sour cream, Cheddar, and lemon juice. Mix until smooth.

5. Butter a 9 x 11-inch baking dish. Lay the broccoli evenly in the dish.

6. When the chicken has cooled a bit, remove from the baking dish and set the cooking liquid aside for the baked rice. Pull the meat from the bones (discard the skin and bones), shred the chicken, and lay it on the broccoli.

7. Pour the soup mixture over the chicken and sprinkle the top with the Parmesan and paprika. Bake until bubbling and golden on top, 30 to 40 minutes. Serve over the baked rice.

BAKED RICE

> **2 cups white rice**
> **4 cups chicken broth (or the reserved cooking liquid from Chicken Divan)**
> **Salt and freshly ground black pepper**

1. Preheat the oven to 350°F.

2. In a 4-quart baking dish, combine the rice, chicken broth, and salt and pepper to taste. Cover and bake until the rice is tender, 35 to 45 minutes.

THE HAPPY COOKBOOK
158

SPAGHETTI BUNDT

My mom always made too much macaroni, because she knew that the next Depression could happen *this very afternoon,* and she'd save all the leftovers and repurpose them later. She'd stir up a couple eggs with lots of cheese, throw in some leftover noodles, bake for half an hour, and that was lunch.

These days we make this with freshly cooked spaghetti (it's only a dollar a box). And now we also bake it in a Bundt cake pan, after hearing a neighbor tell us how the Bundt cake pan had changed her life. No joke. She made Jell-O, breads, cakes, and appetizers, and even flipped it upside down and used that thing in the middle to impale a roast chicken, à la beer butt chicken . . . I mean beer *Bundt* chicken.

I'm jealous she had to wash only one pan.

Cooking spray
1½ cups shredded Fontina, mozzarella, or
  provolone cheese
1½ cups shredded Cheddar cheese (white
  Cheddar is prettier, but yellow works,
  too)
1 cup grated Parmesan cheese
3 large eggs

1½ cups milk, at room temperature
1½ teaspoons salt
1¼ teaspoons freshly ground black pepper
1 pound spaghetti, cooked
One 24-ounce jar marinara sauce, warmed

1. Preheat the oven to 425°F. Coat a Bundt pan with cooking spray.

2. In a large bowl, combine the cheeses, eggs, milk, salt, and pepper and mix until smooth. Add the spaghetti and stir until the cheese mixture is evenly mixed throughout.

3. Use tongs to carefully transfer the noodle mixture to the Bundt pan. Rap it on the countertop a couple times to remove any air bubbles.

4. Bake until golden brown around the edges, about 30 minutes.

5. Using oven mitts, invert a serving plate on top of the pan, then carefully flip the pan over so that the noodle ring plops down on the serving plate. Cut and serve as you would a Bundt cake, but with a drizzle of marinara over the top of each piece.

BALSAMIC BEEF FILETS

•MAKES 6 SERVINGS•

Kathy and I got engaged at table 52 at the legendary Palm Restaurant in Washington, DC. If we went out to eat, we went to the Palm. When Peter was born, Tommy Jacomo, who ran the place, showed up at the hospital the next day with a lobster that was Peter's birth weight: seven pounds eleven ounces. Back then that would have cost the same as a Mercedes payment.

When Peter was big enough for his first dinner at a restaurant, we took him there. Unfortunately he started screaming, so Kathy excused herself from the table and took him into the coatroom, where we thought all that hanging outerwear would surely deaden the sound. It did not. By this point we'd decided it wasn't worth further reputational damage and as we were collecting our coats we heard a woman behind us observe, "There's nothing as beautiful as the sound of a baby crying."

I looked at Kathy and she looked at me, and we rolled our eyes, but at exactly that moment, Peter stopped crying. Shocked, we realized that the woman was Angie Dickinson, the TV and movie star, and she was standing with Larry King, then the king of cable, who was probably thinking, *I'm on a date with Angie Dickinson, somebody look at me!* As we left the coatroom, I left Larry King a dollar tip.

We are a steak and potato family, and this recipe is a favorite inspired by our many nights at the Palm. It's a snap to make, and the hint of rosemary and the balsamic marinade give it such a unique flavor that everybody always asks, "What's in that?" You don't have to ask . . . here it is!

½ cup extra-virgin olive oil
¼ cup balsamic vinegar
¼ cup dry red wine
½ cup chopped shallots
1 garlic clove, minced
2 tablespoons fresh rosemary leaves
Six 8-ounce beef tenderloin steaks
Salt and freshly ground black pepper

1. In a blender, combine the olive oil, vinegar, wine, shallots, garlic, and rosemary and blend until nice and smooth. Pour the marinade into a resealable bag, add the steaks, and seal. Give the bag a good shake and refrigerate for at least 6 hours, squishing the bag around once or twice during that time.

2. Get the grill roaring to medium-high heat. Salt and pepper the steaks to your liking. Set the steaks on the center of the grill for an even temperature and grill on both sides to your desired doneness. We prefer them done to medium and take them off the grill when the interior temperature is almost to 160°F. Let the steaks rest for 10 minutes off the grill before serving.

Pictured with Sally's
Side Salad (page 60)

ROB'S SPICY CREAMY DEER PIG

Our friend Rob is a gracious guest, and as it turns out he can cook. This is one of his favorite recipes, and he calls it Spicy Creamy Deer Pig because exactly like its name, it contains a jalapeño, a chunk of cream cheese, and some venison wrapped in bacon, grilled to perfection.

Rob admits that these roll-ups started as a "recipe of necessity," created from a combination of whatever was left in his refrigerator. Instead of venison you could always substitute a little strip of beef steak; then you could call it "Spicy Creamy Steer Pig." But you have to admit it, deer sounds cooler.

1 pound venison steak or loin (or beef steak)
½ cup A.1. Steak Sauce
½ cup Worcestershire sauce
1 cup store-bought Italian vinaigrette
12 slices bacon
3 ounces (6 tablespoons) cream cheese
Twelve 1-inch-square sections jalapeño (or the chili pepper of your choice), seeds removed

1. On a cutting board, slice the meat into 12 strips 3 to 4 inches long, 1 inch wide, and ¼ to ½ inch thick. Set aside.

2. In a medium bowl, whisk together the A.1., Worcestershire, and vinaigrette. Pour into a resealable plastic bag and add the meat. Slosh around so it's all coated and refrigerate for at least 1 hour (overnight is okay).

3. Here's your mission: You're going to stack a little pile of delicious things on top of each other and then roll them up. To make a single roll-up, first, lay a slice of bacon flat on a surface. Next, place a piece of the marinated meat lengthwise at one end of the bacon (it will not be the same length), then spread ½ tablespoon cream cheese on top of that meat. Place a piece of jalapeño on the cheese. Starting at the end of the bacon with the meat/cheese/pepper stack, roll to the end of the bacon, then push a toothpick through to keep it together. Repeat to make the rest of the roll-ups.

4. Preheat a grill to medium-high heat. Grill the roll-ups until the meat is cooked through and the bacon is browned and crispy.

5. It's okay to serve with the toothpicks still in place, because your spicy creamy deer pig may unravel, and you don't want that.

Merry Christmas

Mary, Peter, Sally, Kathy & Steve Doocy

HOLIDAY RECIPES

SOMETIMES IT'S BEST THAT HOLIDAYS HAP-
pen only once a year.

Lea Thompson was for decades the legendary consumer correspondent at NBC. She was also famous for inviting colleagues who didn't have family nearby to her house on the holidays. In the years before I got married, I was invited to Thanksgiving with the Thompsons.

A lavish spread of snacks always greeted us as we watched Lea put the finishing touches on the turkey, and then her husband, Durke, lifted it into the oven for a four-hour roasting. To pass the time we ate those snacks, played Trivial Pursuit, and talked office politics. The Thompson girls would put on wonderful shows they'd written for the day, and of course there was always a touch football game in the yard.

It was after the football game that we'd return to the kitchen for the turkey unveiling. On one occasion, as we grabbed a beverage and prepared ourselves to be wowed by the bird, Durke opened

the door, and paused—oddly. He said nothing. A curious reporter, I bent over and took a peek. The turkey was the wrong color. That's when Lea crouched down and reported to us in her famous TV voice: "We didn't turn on the oven."

Here's the thing—somebody had also forgotten to turn on the oven *one year before*. Luckily last time they'd had steaks in the freezer.

So Lea did the normal TV thing: She ad libbed. They cut the turkey apart, scooped out the dressing, and turned the oven up really high, and dinner was served late that night. It was perfect. And the next year the turkey was roasting *when we arrived*.

Lea gave us a great story that we still share. After all, you'd think America's number one consumer reporter would remember to roast the turkey on Turkey Day, right? But she's like all of us in the kitchen . . . human.

That kind of thing can happen on any day, but it's especially tough on Thanksgiving, which has a lot of built-in angst for home cooks to make sure that everything is exactly the same as it was the year before. There's something about carrying on family traditions, even though sometimes the recipes we've been eating for decades aren't so good. Why do we still make them? Because we always have and always will. They're part of the fabric of our family. Who cares if nobody eats the cranberries? It's not Thanksgiving without them.

Then there's gravy. We don't eat much of it unless it's a holiday, and the gold standard when it came to gravy was my mom's. I couldn't replicate what proportion of drippings to stock and how much salt and pepper she put in it, because she never used a measuring cup or spoon. I think she probably made it the same way her mom did

President Reagan's Easter Egg Roll, 1987.

in the 1950s, as the short-order cook at Frank and Ems out on the highway in Algona, Iowa.

Whenever I wanted to make mashed potatoes with gravy for that taste of home, I would call my mom in Kansas, and she would walk me through how she did it. I probably called her fifty times, and by about the fifty-first time I'd figured out how to make a good gravy, so maybe I was using it as an excuse to call and show her that even though I was forty years old, a son will always need his mother.

My mom died on Christmas morning 1997. It was sudden and unexpected.

Two weeks after the funeral, I was back home in New Jersey. It was a Sunday morning, and I was the lector for the 10 a.m. mass. They asked me if I wanted a substitute, given what had happened, but I said no, I wanted to do it. In between readings, probably still in shock, standing in church, it was impossible not to think about my mother and wonder about Heaven and all of those things that we hope really do exist. Listening to the choir on the opposite side of the church, I started looking in their direction and noticed in front of the altar an elaborate display of Christmas flowers and gifts and foods.

It took a moment to register, but the closest bouquet to me was a huge spray of daisies. I'd never seen daisies in my church, but there they were, just like the ones Mom held as she walked down the aisle of another church when she married my dad.

Was that a sign? *Maybe daisies are used a lot in churches and I just never noticed*, I said to myself as I eyed the rest of the display. But then I stopped and stared at something you *never* see in the front of any church. Gravy.

A single packet of McCormick gravy mix.

I got goose bumps.

My mom's flowers and gravy packet.

Thanksgiving: Keep calm and baste on.

Maybe the daisies were a sign, and the gravy was another, in case I didn't believe the first one.

It's hard to explain the feeling that washed over me. After a really lousy Christmas, maybe it was a sign from God or Mom that there was a Heaven, and she was up there keeping an eye on me.

You may notice that we didn't print a gravy recipe in this book. It's not that Mom took the recipe with her; I know exactly how to make it. . . .

Remove the meat from the pan and leave a few pan drippings. Over low heat stir in a slurry of 2 tablespoons of cornstarch mixed with 1 or 2 cups of broth. Whisk while it cooks. Salt, pepper, serve.

I have not made it in twenty years, but please try it, it's delicious.

Somebody said once that a legacy is not leaving something *for* people, it's leaving something *in* people.

My mom's gravy? As I tap on my chest, just know it's right in there.

MARY'S CHRISTMAS FRENCH TOAST CASSEROLE

Kathy had a roommate named Mary Finnegan, a flight attendant for American Airlines. In the 1980s Mary had a boyfriend who they nicknamed "Skylab," because you never knew when he was going to drop in.

The roomies never cooked then, but years later when Mary's kids were in college she gave us this recipe and we started a tradition, making it on Christmas Eve, so that the kids would wake up Christmas morning to the sweet smell of French toasty apples, knowing that Santa had been there overnight. (We still make it randomly throughout the year, just to confuse the kids.)

8 tablespoons (1 stick) butter, melted, plus more for the baking dish
1 cup packed light brown sugar
3 teaspoons ground cinnamon
3 Granny Smith apples, peeled, cored, quartered, and cut into ⅛-inch-thick slices
½ cup chopped pecans
6 large eggs
1½ cups whole milk
1 teaspoon pure vanilla extract
One 16-ounce loaf cinnamon bread, cut into 1-inch squares (we use Pepperidge Farms Cinnamon Swirl)
Whipped cream, for serving

1. Generously butter a 9 x 12-inch (or similar size) baking dish.

2. In a large bowl, combine the brown sugar, 1 teaspoon of the cinnamon, and the melted butter and stir until smooth.

3. Place the apples in a microwave-safe bowl with 1 tablespoon water, cover with plastic wrap, and microwave for 60 seconds to soften.

4. Drain the apples and add them to the brown sugar/butter mixture. Add the pecans and mix until evenly coated.

5. Pour the mixture into the prepared baking dish and spread it out neatly.

6. In a large bowl, whisk the eggs, then whisk in the milk, vanilla, and remaining 2 teaspoons cinnamon to combine. Add the bread cubes to the bowl and stir until the liquid is completely absorbed.

7. Pour the bread mixture evenly into the baking dish over the brown sugar/apple/nuts layer.

8. Cover the dish with foil and refrigerate overnight. The next morning, uncover the dish and let it come to room temperature.

9. Preheat the oven to 375°F.

10. Cover again with foil and bake for 45 minutes or until set. Remove the foil and bake another 5 minutes to brown it a bit.

11. Run a knife around the edge of the casserole to loosen, then invert a large serving platter on top and flip the French toast out onto the platter. Let it rest at least 5 minutes before serving.

12. Cut into a dozen squares, spatula it out, and serve with whipped cream. We leave this on the counter for a few hours on Christmas, because you never know who'll drop in.

DEVILED EGGS

Our mothers made this classic recipe as a way to do something practical with the two dozen perfectly good Easter eggs we could find after our annual living room egg hunt. Notice I said the eggs we *could* find, not *would* . . . my mom found one blue egg under the couch in our house in Salina, Kansas, three years after we stopped having egg hunts. She'd been complaining about an odd odor in that corner for years, but everybody just assumed it was Dad.

Fast-forward to today, and we are at a fancy dinner party in Palm Beach; when the waitress comes around with the appetizer course, it is this exact recipe!

I was talking deviled egg recipes with Paula Deen, who had a suggestion for keeping them cool for a picnic. Don't overfill them; and when you pack them up, take two prepared egg halves and stick them together the way they were before you cut the egg in half, then wrap your "egg" in plastic wrap. Much more mobile, too. Great idea—thanks, Paula!

We serve these at *every* family holiday dinner.

6 large eggs, hard-boiled and peeled
3 tablespoons mayo (we love Duke's)
½ teaspoon mustard powder
Salt and freshly ground black pepper
Optional mix-ins (choose only one!):
    horseradish, pickle relish, finely diced
    cooked bacon, for minced fresh dill
Sweet paprika, for garnish

1. Halve the eggs lengthwise and pop the yellow yolks into a bowl.
2. Add the mayo, mustard powder, ⅛ teaspoon salt, a couple shakes of pepper, and an optional mix-in and use a fork to mash everything together. When the filling is creamy smooth, taste and adjust with more salt and pepper as needed. Spoon the filling back into the egg whites (if you want to get fancy, use a pastry bag and swirl in just enough to rise above the egg).
3. Give a shake of paprika on the eggs just before you serve them. If you put it on too early, it's not as pretty.

KATHY'S COFFEE AND COINTREAU CRANBERRY SAUCE

• MAKES 6 TO 8 SERVINGS •

During the early years of our marriage, we were invited to a friend's Thanksgiving party, and when we asked the host if we could bring anything, thinking they would say, "No, just bring your appetite!" they shocked us by saying, "Yes, bring the cranberry sauce."

Kathy loves an assignment, and because she'd never made cranberry *anything*, she asked around, and one friend who worked overnight hours for the Pentagon offered up this eye-opening recipe. We've now made this for thirty Thanksgivings, and people always ask what gives it that punch. The answer: coffee and Cointreau.

2 large pears
2 lemons
2 cups strong coffee
1½ cups sugar
One 12-ounce package fresh cranberries,
    picked over and rinsed
1 cinnamon stick
2 tablespoons orange liqueur (we use
    Cointreau)
1 tablespoon grated orange zest, for garnish

1. Peel, core, and quarter the pears and place them in a medium bowl. Squeeze the juice of 2 lemons into the bowl and gently toss to coat the pears so they don't turn brown. Set aside.

2. In a medium saucepan, combine the coffee and ½ cup of the sugar. Stir and bring to a simmer over medium heat. Place the pear quarters in the saucepan (let the lemon juice drip off) and poach the pears for up to 20 minutes or until soft. Set the pan aside to let the pears cool in the coffee mixture.

3. In a separate medium saucepan, combine the cranberries, 1 cup water, the remaining 1 cup sugar, and the cinnamon stick. Bring to a boil over medium heat. Reduce the heat to a simmer and cook until the liquid thickens into a syrup, at least 10 minutes. Set the pan off the heat to cool.

4. When the cranberry mixture is no longer hot, remove and discard the cinnamon stick and stir in the orange liqueur. Drain the pears, cut them into ¾-inch chunks, and add them to the cranberries. Give a gentle stir and pour the cranberry sauce into a medium serving bowl.

5. Garnish with the orange zest, cover, and chill until serving.

THANKSGIVING DRESSING

This dressing is a combination of the way Kathy's mother made it plus some tasty additives from her lifelong friend Joan Keyloun. It also smells exactly like my mom's dressing, but when my mother made hers, she would chop up the various organ meats and other goodies that came packed inside the turkey and stir them into the dressing. At least once a meal, I'd shovel in a big forkful of dressing covered with gravy, only to discover that I had about a quarter-pound of *turkey liver in my mouth!*

Once I was in my teens, I offered to help my mother make the dressing, which meant that when it was time to add the "bonus organ meats," I'd insist she set them aside for my father, who would happily eat them. Dad loved necks, livers, gizzards—all those things that most of us place directly in the garbage. Mom would cook them up separately and place them on Dad's plate. The 1960s were like that. . . .

Anyway, no "surprises" in this, just the great traditional taste of sausage and dressing.

> 2 tablespoons butter, plus more for the baking dish
> 1 pound pork sausage, crumbled (we use Jimmy Dean)
> 1 large yellow onion, finely diced
> 4 celery stalks, finely diced
> One 14-ounce package stuffing mix (we use Pepperidge Farm)
> 2 cups chicken broth

> 2 large eggs, lightly whisked
> ½ cup raisins
> ¾ cup slivered almonds
> ½ cup chopped fresh flat-leaf parsley, plus a sprig for garnish
> ½ teaspoon salt
> ½ teaspoon freshly ground black pepper

1. Preheat the oven to 350°F. Butter a 9 x 13-inch baking dish.

2. In a large soup pot, cook the sausage over medium-high heat, breaking it up as you cook it, until almost done, about 10 minutes. Add the butter, onion, and celery and cook until the onion is golden and the sausage is cooked, about 5 minutes. Remove from the heat.

3. Add the stuffing mix, broth, eggs, raisins, almonds, parsley, salt, and pepper and mix until the stuffing is soft and evenly moistened. Transfer the dressing to the prepared baking dish, spread it out evenly, and cover with foil.

4. Place in the oven (see Note) and bake for 45 minutes, then remove the foil. Bake until the top is golden brown, at least 15 minutes more. Garnish with a big, beautiful sprig of parsley. Once it's done, let Thanksgiving begin!

NOTE: *Timing-wise, try to put the dressing in the oven when the turkey has only a half hour to go. That way the dressing should be done about the time the finished turkey has rested before slicing.*

DR. OZ'S SPICED MASHED SWEET POTATOES WITH POMEGRANATES

TV's Dr. Oz says this is his favorite food, especially over the holidays.

We love his wife Lisa's cookbooks and listen to her on Oprah Radio, and this is a recipe she has perfected during their marriage. She tells us, "Candied sweet potatoes were always a standard at holiday gatherings, but over time our taste buds grew up, and we wanted something a little more sophisticated. This version has a fragrant blend of spices with just a hint of honey. The crunch of pomegranate seeds gives interest to the otherwise smooth-textured dish."

We agree completely, Lisa—it has such a unique blend of tastes that you just have to stop and go *wow*. This Thanksgiving we added it to our table, and because the kids were so interested in those beautiful pomegranate seeds on the top, it was the first bowl emptied and put in the dishwasher.

**4 medium orange-fleshed sweet potatoes/
 yams (about 10 ounces each)**
1 tablespoon coconut oil, melted

1 teaspoon honey
½ teaspoon pomegranate molasses
½ teaspoon ground cinnamon
⅛ teaspoon ground cardamom
Fine sea salt
**½ cup pomegranate seeds (arils),
 from ½ pomegranate**

1. Position a rack in the center of the oven and preheat the oven to 400°F.

2. Pierce each sweet potato a few times with a fork. Place them on a rimmed baking sheet and bake until the potatoes are tender when pierced with the tip of a small sharp knife, about 45 minutes.

3. Using a kitchen towel to protect your hands, peel the sweet potatoes and transfer the flesh to a medium bowl. Mash the sweet potatoes with a potato masher or a large fork. Mix in the coconut oil, honey, pomegranate molasses, cinnamon, and cardamom. Season with salt to taste. Transfer to a serving bowl, top with the pomegranate seeds, and serve.

TANYA AND ALAN THICKE'S TURKEY

I first met Alan Thicke about thirty years ago, when I was hosting *House Party* on NBC. He was one of the biggest TV stars in the world, and it was humbling that he came to watch me do my show. Years later, Alan and I played tennis at the Chris Evert Pro Celebrity Tennis Classic in Boca Raton. He was a real competitor, and he knew the quickest way to score was to hit the ball directly to me. Loved that guy. That night, Alan, his wife, Tanya, and Kathy and I had a wonderful dinner talking about our families.

After Alan died, we were having dinner with Tanya and she told us something we didn't know about him—that his happiest meal of the year was always turkey. Why? Tanya says Alan loved the holiday season, and the smell of the bird baking made him euphoric. Tanya would make this recipe (her mother's) not just for Christmas, but also for both US and Canadian Thanksgivings and sometimes for his birthday.

So here's a recipe that made one of TV's funniest fathers happy for many years. We love it because it is so juicy and tender, thanks to the vermouth. You can slice it thin, but we like it Thicke.

One 15-pound turkey
5 cups vermouth
2 small oranges, peeled and separated into
   segments
1 yellow onion, peeled and quartered

8 tablespoons (1 stick) unsalted butter, at
   room temperature
½ cup extra-virgin olive oil
Salt and freshly ground black pepper
Seasonings of your family's choice

1. Place the turkey in a brining bag. Pour 3 cups of the vermouth over the bird, zip the bag closed, and place the turkey breast side down in a shallow roasting pan. Marinate in the refrigerator overnight.

2. The next day, preheat the oven to 400°F.

3. Drain the vermouth and stuff the turkey with the oranges and onion. Smear the butter all over the outside of the turkey. Pour the remaining 2 cups vermouth over the turkey, then pour the olive oil over the bird. Sprinkle on your family's favorite seasonings—salt and pepper is a good start.

4. Roast for 30 minutes, then reduce the heat to 350°F. Cover the turkey with foil and roast for 1 hour. Uncover and baste with the pan juices. Then continue to roast until the turkey registers 165°F in the thickest part of the thigh and under the wing. The total roasting time will vary according to the size of your turkey and accuracy of your oven, so start checking on the bird after 2½ hours.

5. Remove the turkey from the oven, cover it with foil, and let rest 30 minutes before carving.

SUNDAY GRAVY

Before we knew him, our friend Erik Pettersen left New York for South Florida to take care of his ailing mother, and they would watch *Fox & Friends* together in the morning as he made her a little breakfast. He said to me the first time we met, "Steve, you were like Mike Wallace—every time we turned on the TV, we knew you'd be there." He said because they spent every weekday morning with me, they considered me a friend.

One of the things Erik and his mom talked about was how one day when she got better, they would take all of the experience he'd gotten working in some of New York's best restaurants and open their own place in Florida. He'd do the cooking and she would handle the business. A beautiful dream for a mother and son.

After his mother passed, Erik did open his own restaurant, Evo Italian in Tequesta, Florida, at a location his mother said would be a winner— and it is. The recipes are Erik's interpretation of his mother's and grandmother's Sicilian classics, and none is better than his Sunday gravy. Kathy makes this for holiday weekends when our family is together under one roof and we want something special that you don't have every day.

As for calling this gravy, it is clearly not the thin beige-brown gravy I grew up with in Kansas, because it's tomato-y red and packed with tender, juicy meats. Then again, growing up in Kansas I remember gravy was sometimes served at many *salad bars*. Don't know why, but there it was.

I also recall watching *The Godfather* in 1972, as Clemenza the capo—who said, "Leave the gun, take the cannoli"—showed Michael Corleone how to make a meaty tomato sauce that looks a lot like this. When I saw it, I thought it looked unbelievably great. And now that we make a version of it, we know it is. Of course that's the same film in which Don Corleone said, "Revenge is a dish best served cold...."

This recipe is a dish best served hot and over pasta.

1 cup extra-virgin olive oil
1 pound pork belly or fat back
1 pound Angus beef chuck roast or boneless beef short ribs (cut into 2-inch cubes)
1 pound boneless pork butt (shoulder), cut into 2-inch cubes
1 pound sweet Italian sausage links
2 large Spanish onions, cut into ½-inch chunks
8 garlic cloves, smashed with the side of a knife and peeled
3 tablespoons sea salt, plus more for the pasta water
1½ cups drinkable Chardonnay
Six 28-ounce cans whole Italian San Marzano tomatoes (certified D.O.P.)
3 tablespoons red pepper flakes
2 pounds mezze rigatoni
½ pound Pecorino Romano cheese
8 ounces whipped ricotta cheese, for topping
1 cup fresh basil leaves

1. In a *big* saucepan or stockpot, heat the olive oil over medium-high heat. Add the pork belly or fat back and sear it on all sides to release the juices. Add the beef, pork, and sausage and brown the meats to seal in the flavor, turning to sear all sides, 10 to 15 minutes total. Add the onions and garlic and cook until nicely browned and caramelized, 3 to 5 minutes, but don't let them burn. Add 1 tablespoon of the salt and pour in the wine to deglaze the pan and bring all the flavors together. Cook until the wine has reduced by half, 10 to 15 minutes.

2. Pour the cans of tomatoes into a large bowl and crush the tomatoes by hand.

3. Add the tomatoes to the pot, cover, reduce the heat to low, and simmer for 6½ to 8 hours. Taste a piece of pork for tenderness. If it falls apart, it's ready. Add the remaining 2 tablespoons salt and the red pepper flakes.

4. When you're ready to eat, bring a large pot of salted water to a boil. Add the rigatoni and cook until al dente. Drain and pour the pasta onto a large platter. Place the tender chunks of meat on top, then the pasta sauce. Dust the top with plenty of Romano. Dollop the whipped ricotta in the middle of the sauce, then tear the basil leaves into pieces over the entire dish.

HANNITY'S CORNED BEEF AND CABBAGE

When Sean Hannity was twelve, he worked as a dishwasher at the Norwood Inn in West Hempstead, New York. He was making $2.25 an hour. The boss could see Sean was a driven teenager and he needed help on the grill, so he promoted him to cook and gave him a fifty-cent raise. That's where Sean learned how to cook lobster and steak, make burgers, and bake cakes— all the things on a big menu he could make, and make fast. Of those thousands of orders he filled, this is his favorite recipe. "It's just delicious," he told me, "and make sure you eat the fatty layer first!"

True to his Irish roots, Hannity says it's a simple recipe that anyone can pull off. So why wait for St. Patrick's Day, the day everybody pretends they're Irish? Think outside the cabbage and try it now.

Hannitize your kitchen!

2½- to 3-pound corned beef brisket, with spice packet
1 small yellow onion, peeled and halved
1 teaspoon minced garlic
4 large potatoes, peeled and quartered
1 pound baby carrots
1 small cabbage head, cored and cut into 5 or 6 wedges
2 tablespoons butter
Salt and freshly ground black pepper

1. Place the corned beef fatty side up in a Dutch oven. Shake the spice packet that came with the brisket over the meat (if there wasn't one, use 2 tablespoons pickling spices). Place the onion alongside the meat and sprinkle in the garlic. Add enough water to easily cover the meat. (When Kathy makes it she puts in a bottle of Guinness Stout along with the water. I like anything that stimulates the Irish economy.) Place the pot over high heat and bring the liquid to a boil. Reduce the heat to low, cover the pot, and simmer for 2 hours.

2. Add the potatoes and carrots and simmer for 30 minutes.

3. Add the cabbage. You may need to remove some of the very hot water to make way for the cabbage; if so, use a Pyrex measuring cup and carefully remove enough to accommodate the cabbage wedges. Simmer until the cabbage is softened and the potatoes are done, about 15 minutes.

4. Remove the corned beef and vegetables to a serving platter. Dot the vegetables with little dabs of butter and sprinkle on salt and pepper to taste.

5. Cut the fatty layer from the brisket and slice the meat against the grain. Serve with the vegetables.

ELENA'S LEMON CAKE

Behind this cake is one of our favorite stories in this cookbook. If you haven't read the opening to the Desserts chapter on page 200, do—and you'll learn why this cake could change your life.

LEMON FILLING
1½ cups granulated sugar
6 tablespoons cornstarch
¼ teaspoon salt
½ cup fresh lemon juice
3 large egg yolks, whisked well
1½ cups boiling water
2 teaspoons grated lemon zest

CAKE
Crisco, for the cake pan
1 cup flour, plus a dusting for the cake pan
6 large eggs, separated
1 teaspoon baking powder
Pinch of salt
1 cup granulated sugar
1 teaspoon pure vanilla extract

ICING AND TOPPING
2 cups powdered sugar
1 teaspoon fresh lemon juice
1 pint fresh strawberries, hulled and halved
    from top to bottom

1. To make the lemon filling: Sift the granulated sugar, cornstarch, and salt into a heavy saucepan. Blend in ½ cup cold water and the lemon juice. Set over medium-low heat and whisk until smooth (do not boil). Add the egg yolks and whisk thoroughly. Stir constantly with a wooden spoon until thickened, 5 to 7 minutes. Add the boiling water, stir a few minutes, and the mixture will be much thicker. Remove from the heat and stir in the lemon zest. Pour into a bowl, cover with plastic wrap, and refrigerate for at least 1 hour, until completely cool.

2. In the meantime, make the cake: Preheat the oven to 350°F. Grease a 9 x 9-inch cake pan with Crisco, dust the pan with flour, and line the bottom with wax paper.

3. In a stand mixer, whisk the egg whites on high speed until foamy and soft peaks start to form (like a meringue). Pour into a large bowl and set aside.

4. Sift the 1 cup flour, baking powder, and salt into a large bowl.

5. Back in the mixer, beat the egg yolks and sugar on high speed until lemony colored. Add the flour mixture and vanilla to the mixer and beat until smooth. Use a spatula to fold the foamy egg whites into the batter until smooth.

6. Pour the batter into the prepared cake pan and bake until golden brown and a toothpick inserted in the center comes out clean, about 35 minutes. Invert the cake onto a cooling rack and let it cool completely.

7. Using a long serrated knife or a wire cake cutter, cut the cake horizontally to make 2 even layers. Place the bottom layer on a serving platter and slather the cooled lemon filling over the top, as much as you like (the filling recipe makes a big batch). We like about ¾ inch of filling (if you're clever with a cutter and can cut 3 layers, there's actually enough filling for a bottom and middle layer). Smooth out the filling and lay on the top cake layer.

8. To make the icing: In a large bowl, combine the powdered sugar, lemon juice, and 2 to 3 tablespoons water. Mix until smooth. If needed, add more water a tablespoon at a time to achieve a uniform consistency.

9. Frost the top and sides of the cake immediately, then place the strawberries in single file around the edge of the cake, forming a strawberry square. Now it's time to serve. Store in the fridge.

BETTY'S BOURBON PUMPKIN CHEESECAKE

Our friend Martha MacCallum's mom, Betty, passed this recipe down to her daughter after she found it in the early 1980s, although they adapted it over the years as times and tastes changed. Martha says, "You can make it the day before Thanksgiving and it sits on the counter looking like an amazing superstar, and you can say, 'Yes, I made it myself!' It smells scrumptious and has bourbon in it, which sinks into the crust. Need I say more?"

CRUST
Butter, for the pan
¾ cup graham cracker crumbs
½ cup finely chopped pecans
¼ cup packed light brown sugar
¼ cup granulated sugar
4 tablespoons (½ stick) unsalted butter, melted and cooled

FILLING
1½ cups canned unsweetened pumpkin puree (not pumpkin pie filling)
3 large eggs
1½ teaspoons ground cinnamon
½ teaspoon freshly grated nutmeg
½ teaspoon ground ginger
½ teaspoon salt
½ cup packed light brown sugar
Three 8-ounce packages cream cheese, cut into bits
½ cup granulated sugar
2 tablespoons heavy cream
1 tablespoon cornstarch
1 tablespoon bourbon
1 teaspoon pure vanilla extract

TOPPING
2 cups sour cream
2 tablespoons granulated sugar
1 tablespoon bourbon

16 pecan halves, for garnish

1. To make the crust: Butter a 9-inch springform pan. In a large bowl, combine the crumbs, pecans, and sugars. Stir in the melted butter and press into the bottom and halfway up the sides of the prepared pan. Chill the crust for 1 hour.

2. Meanwhile, make the filling: Position a rack in the center of the oven and preheat the oven to 350°F.

3. In a medium bowl, whisk together the pumpkin, eggs, spices, salt, and brown sugar until combined. In a large bowl, with an electric mixer, cream the cream cheese, sugar, heavy cream, cornstarch, bourbon, and vanilla. Add the pumpkin mixture and beat until smooth. Pour the filling into the crust.

4. Bake until the center is set, 55 minutes to 1 hour. Remove from the oven and let cool in the pan on a rack for about 5 minutes while you make the topping (but leave the oven on).

5. To make the topping: In a medium bowl, whisk together the sour cream, granulated sugar, and bourbon. Spread it over the cheesecake and return to the oven to bake for 5 minutes.

6. Let the cake cool completely on the rack, then cover and refrigerate overnight to chill. Carefully remove the side of the pan, garnish the top with the pecan halves, and serve.

CANDY CANES

These cookies prompt some of Sally's happiest childhood Christmas memories. Of course all the kids wanted Santa to have a delicious snack when he stopped by our house to deliver their mother lode of presents. Any cookies would suffice, but Sally thought he'd like these cookies because she'd seen in all of the Santa movies that the North Pole was rich in candy cane décor.

What the kids didn't know is that we ate the cookies after they went to bed and left Santa a treat he really wanted . . . a dirty martini with three olives. When the kids came down on Christmas morning, the cookies were always gone and that empty martini glass was found in the sink.

1 cup sugar
1 cup vegetable shortening (Crisco is a
    classic where I come from)
½ cup milk
½ teaspoon pure vanilla extract
½ teaspoon peppermint extract
1 large egg
3½ cups flour
1 teaspoon baking powder
¼ teaspoon salt
½ teaspoon red food coloring
3 tablespoons granulated or powdered
    sugar

1. In a stand mixer, combine the sugar, shortening, milk, vanilla, peppermint, and egg and beat on low speed until smooth. Keep the mixer on low and slowly add the flour, baking powder, and salt. Blend until smooth.

2. Take the dough out of the bowl and cut it in half. Roll half into a ball, wrap it in plastic, and put it in the refrigerator. Place the other half of the dough back in the mixer bowl. Turn the mixer to low and drip in the food coloring a little at a time, until the color is as you want it for your candy canes and it's blended smoothly.

3. Remove the dough, roll it into a ball, wrap it in plastic, and refrigerate for at least 20 minutes.

4. Remove both dough balls from the fridge. Tear a small amount of white dough (about a rounded teaspoon) and roll it into a ball that is a little under 1 inch wide. Set it on a piece of wax paper or parchment paper on a plate and repeat until all the white dough has been rolled into balls. Place the plate in the refrigerator to firm up the balls.

5. Repeat with the red dough. Refrigerate the red balls for at least 20 minutes.

6. Position a rack in the center of the oven and preheat the oven to 375°F.

7. Set a large piece of wax paper or parchment paper on a flat surface. Take a red ball and a white ball and roll each into a snake about 4 inches long.

Lay the red snakes next to the white snakes, and give them a gentle roll in the same direction to fuse them together into a tube. Next, carefully twist the red and white tube so it resembles a candy cane, curving the top of the cookie to make a hook. Once twisted, if one tube is longer than the other, trim the end with a butter knife. Repeat to make the rest of the candy canes, setting them about 1 inch apart on an ungreased baking sheet as you work.

8. Bake until the edges start to brown, about 10 minutes. Sprinkle the hot cookies with granulated or powdered sugar (experiment to see which you prefer; we like them both).

9. Let the cookies cool before Santa gets his snack. And if you keep them refrigerated in a resealable bag they should be good for a couple days.

"Santa won't miss one . . ."

GINGERBREAD COOKIES

The mother of a local preschooler was organizing a holiday party and sent a note home to every family that they were responsible for bringing four dozen cookies to the event. And there was a stipulation: The cookies had to be homemade. Realizing this was a competition to see which mom could make the best homemade cookies, Kathy asked around for a recipe. She found one but couldn't follow it exactly because we didn't have a mixer at the time, so she tried it using a food processor and accidentally added too much of one ingredient. Several moms asked her what gave the cookies that special taste, and she said, "I measured wrong."

That tasty mistake of adding a little extra ground ginger is now part of Kathy's official gingerbread cookie recipe.

By the way, from what I saw, only about half the parents actually baked homemade cookies from their family kitchens—unless the other half were heirs to the Keebler fortune.

2 sticks (½ pound) butter, at room
    temperature
1½ cups sugar
⅓ cup molasses
1 large egg
2¼ cups all-purpose flour, plus more for the
    work surface
1 cup whole wheat flour
2 teaspoons baking soda
2 teaspoons ground ginger

1 teaspoon ground cinnamon
½ teaspoon freshly grated nutmeg
¼ teaspoon ground cloves
¼ teaspoon salt
Store-bought red and green decorating
    icing

1. In a bowl, with an electric mixer, cream the butter and sugar until thoroughly mixed. Add the molasses and egg and blend until smooth.

2. In a medium bowl, combine the flours, baking soda, ginger, cinnamon, nutmeg, cloves, and salt.

3. With the mixer on low, add the flour mixture and blend until you have a smooth dough. Form the dough into a log, wrap it in plastic, and refrigerate for at least 2 hours, but overnight is best.

4. Preheat the oven to 350°F. Line a baking sheet with parchment paper or a silicone baking mat.

5. Lightly flour a work surface and roll out the dough to about a ¼-inch thickness. Using floured cookie cutters, cut out gingerbread people or other desired shapes. Place the cookies about 1 inch apart on the prepared baking sheet.

6. Bake until the edges are set (test with a spatula for crispiness), 6 to 10 minutes.

7. Let the cookies cool a few minutes on the pan, then pull them off the pans on the parchment paper and let them cool completely. Decorate with red and green icing.

GRANDMA LIL'S SNOWBALL COOKIES

·MAKES ABOUT 40 COOKIES·

I grew up with a Swedish grandmother who made spritz butter cookies that she'd shoot out of a gun and then decorate with all sorts of icings and colored sugars. Back then she'd spend weeks baking, and then give them away to friends and family members. Kathy had never seen such a thing when we first got married, and during those early years we'd bake them by the dozen, box them up, and give them as Christmas gifts. Most people assumed we'd bought them at a store and were shocked that we'd made them with our own hands.

But that was twenty years ago, and now it's hard to make any kind of food to give away that will work for everybody. It seems there's always somebody with a gluten, wheat, milk, egg, or nut allergy, and you don't want to make anyone sick as they're eating a happy butter cookie. Now we just give booze.

Kathy's mom, Lil, made these cookies a tradition at their house in Encino, California, where it never snowed. The powdered sugar makes a bit of a mess, but whose house is ever neat and tidy during the holidays? Martha Stewart, put your hand down. . . .

2 cups powdered sugar
2 sticks (½ pound) butter, at room
   temperature
¼ teaspoon salt
2 teaspoon pure vanilla extract
2¼ cups flour
1 cup walnut halves, finely diced

1. In a bowl, with an electric mixer, combine ⅔ cup of the powdered sugar, the butter, salt, and vanilla and beat on medium speed until smooth.

2. Mix in the flour slowly, occasionally scraping down the bowl sides with a spatula if needed. Once blended, toss in the nuts and mix until completely integrated.

3. Divide the dough into 4 portions. Roll each portion of dough into a log, then on parchment paper (or a lightly floured surface) keep rolling it back and forth to create a skinny tube of dough about 1 inch thick and up to 12 inches long. Once you've turned all 4 portions into tubes, carefully wrap them in plastic wrap and refrigerate for about 20 minutes to firm up.

4. Position a rack in the center of the oven and preheat the oven to 375°F.

5. Remove the dough from the fridge and use a butter knife to cut each tube into ¾-inch sections. Use your fingertips to roll the dough sections into 1-inch balls. Place them on an ungreased baking sheet about 1 inch apart.

6. Bake until *slightly* golden. Start watching at 12 minutes; they turn fast.

7. Let the cookies rest on the baking sheet for a few minutes, until slightly cooled but still warm.

8. Pour the remaining 1⅓ cups powdered sugar into a shallow dish. Roll the still-warm balls in the sugar, then let them cool completely on the baking sheet. (Count on tasting a few at this stage, for quality control purposes—they're delicious!)

TOBA'S TASTY CARAMEL APPLE BLOSSOMS

Toba Potosky is the audio guy on *Fox & Friends*, and his long-gone Grandma Fanny still looms large in his life. In fact, he and his wife, Ronni, now live in what was Fanny's Brooklyn apartment. Fond memories surround them of a grandmother's love and many of life's lessons—lessons taught in the kitchen and around the stove. To this day, Fanny's cast-iron frying pan still sits on the stove. It's rarely used these days, but it will never be moved from its place.

Grandma Fanny grew up in the 1920s in upstate New York, the second youngest of ten children, mostly girls. She told Toba that when she and her younger sister, Ruth, would wake up in the morning after one of the older girls had been out on a date with a farm boy, they would go downstairs to the kitchen and see a bushel of apples, which the farm boy had brought to the girl's parents. If two sisters had dates, there'd be two bushels of apples, which certainly meant apple pie, applesauce, and apple cake by evening.

One Thanksgiving, Toba needed a dessert to go with his holiday turkey dinner. He thought about a simple apple pie, which he'd seen Fanny make a hundred times in her kitchen; but she hadn't left a written recipe, so he looked around and found this idea of apple blossoms, which he adapted. They're easy to make and look great when baked.

When he placed his first batch of powdered sugar–dusted apple blossoms on the table, his first thought was *What would Grandma think of this?* Then he realized that he'd placed them on her white oval platter—and concluded that that was her sign of approval.

Apple blossoms are now a Thanksgiving staple at Toba and Ronni's apartment, and at Fox News, because he'll bring in the leftovers to rave reviews.

"I love being in Grandma's kitchen," he says. "Thank you, Grandma Fanny."

Baking spray (with flour)
3 apples, the redder the skin the better, such as Honeycrisp, Gala, or Winesap
Juice of ½ lemon
Two 9 x 14-inch packaged puff pastry sheets, thawed if frozen
Caramel sundae syrup, in a squeeze bottle
¼ cup granulated sugar
1 tablespoon ground cinnamon
Powdered sugar, for serving (optional)
Ice cream or whipped cream, for serving

1. Position a rack in the center of the oven and preheat the oven to 350°F. Coat 6 cups of a muffin tin with baking spray.

2. Core the apples, leaving the skin on. Halve them from top to bottom, then cut each half vertically into ⅛-inch-thick (or even thinner) wedges using a mandoline. As you work, place the apple slices in a bowl of water with the lemon juice to keep them from browning.

3. Unroll one of the puff pastry sheets on parchment paper. Using a rolling pin, you can roll the dough to about ⅛ inch thick, which makes the sheet a little larger.

4. Using a sharp knife or pizza cutter, cut the pastry sheet into 3 thin strips about 3 inches wide and about 14 inches long. Repeat to roll out and cut strips from the second puff pastry sheet.

5. Squeeze out a line of caramel syrup lengthwise down the center of each strip, up to 2 tablespoons per strip.

6. To make each apple blossom, place the apple slices lengthwise along a dough strip, with the red skin rising ¼ to ½ inch above the edge. Overlap the apple slices as you go.

7. Mix the sugar and cinnamon in a small bowl and lightly dust the apples with this mixture.

8. Fold the bottom half of the dough over the apple slices, leaving the red rounded edges of the apple slices exposed. Starting from one end, roll up the dough to form an apple blossom. Place it in a muffin cup. Repeat to make the rest of the apple blossoms. Lightly sprinkle some of the cinnamon sugar over each blossom.

9. Bake until the caramel turns a darker color and starts bubbling up between the rolled pastry dough, about 30 minutes. Check frequently to prevent burning, since ovens can vary in temperature.

10. Set the muffin pan on a rack and let the apple blossoms cool for 5 to 10 minutes. Use a butter knife to loosen the sides and remove the blossoms from the pan. Dust with powdered sugar, if desired, for a spectacular finish.

11. You can serve these just like an apple pie, with ice cream or whipped cream, your choice.

12. Make sure you've taken pictures of yourself making these. Unless you're a master baker, your friends and family may not believe you did it.

SARAH HUCKABEE SANDERS'S BOURBON CHOCOLATE PECAN PIE

This is the most famous pie in the world.

On Thanksgiving 2016, White House Press Secretary Sarah Huckabee Sanders baked it for her family, as she had been doing for years, and proudly Instagrammed her specialty at her husband's family farm. Suddenly she took grief from the Twitterverse and some reporters because it was so perfect that it looked like a stock photo.

Taking the high road, a few weeks later Sarah baked up a batch of pies that looked exactly like the one she'd posted on Instagram and served them to the White House press corps, who reportedly said they were delicious and picture perfect. #PieGate ended.

Now Sarah's secrets can be revealed: She uses good bourbon and a store-bought pie crust, because sometimes life is too short to make crust from scratch. Her final touch? She uses a hammer—not kidding, a real hammer—to crush the pecans in a zip-top bag. "Less mess than a food processor, and a great stress reliever!"

4 large eggs
1 cup light corn syrup
6 tablespoons (¾ stick) butter, melted
½ cup granulated sugar
¼ cup packed light brown sugar
2 to 4 tablespoons bourbon, according to taste (she typically uses Blanton's, Maker's Mark, or Woodford Reserve; if you use really cheap bourbon, you can tell)
1 tablespoon flour
1 tablespoon pure vanilla extract
1 cup finely chopped pecans (placed in a zip-top bag and crushed with a hammer)
1 cup milk chocolate chips
Unbaked pie crust (make your own or use a frozen deep-dish pie crust)
Vanilla ice cream, for serving

1. Position a rack in the lower third of the oven and preheat the oven to 350°F.

2. In a large bowl, combine the eggs, corn syrup, and melted butter and mix until smooth. Add the sugars, bourbon, flour, vanilla, pecans, and chocolate chips, stirring in each one completely before adding the next.

3. Pour the mixture into the pie crust and bake until the crust is browned and the filling is firm and bubbling, about 1 hour, but start watching it closely at 50 minutes, because every oven is different. If it's browning too much on the edges, you may want to take it out a little early.

4. It's best served warm with vanilla ice cream on top!

Photo on pages 196–97.

Sarah Huckabee Sanders's Bourbon
Chocolate Pecan Pie (page 195)

DESSERTS

KATHY AND I ARE IN THE DESSERT STAGE OF our marriage. Our kids are grown; they've got jobs and places of their own. But our lives go on, and now we have lots more time to spend together—again. I'm learning how to golf, and Kathy's learning to play tennis again, since her shoulder replacement. "Didn't hurt my Chardonnay arm," she brags.

Kathy and I knew that by this point in our lives we'd have plenty of recipes and stories to share in a cookbook. But we didn't realize when we started that the process of writing the book would be a family bonding experience.

For a year, we mainly talked about food. And while my kids all know a lot of my life story, they never knew what I ate growing up, because I never talked about it. Sure, people remember watching *The Brady Bunch* or *Gilligan's Island*, but who talks about the foods we ate back in the day, and who still makes them for supper today? We've been

Working out our Chardonnay arms.

doing that at our house all year, and a lot of my childhood favorite recipes are now my kids' favorite foods. Sally asks me twice a week if I'll make my mom's cheesy bierocks.

We turned our house into a test kitchen as we refined the exact measurements that make a recipe taste the way we remember it. In the mornings I'd show iPhone pictures of dinner (yes, we are those people now) or an apple galette or waffle brownie to our producer Gavin, who said more than once he thought this cookbook has been a gift to the Doocy family, "because it's brought your family together around the table again, sharing meals and memories with the people you love most."

And then he told me this story.

Gavin's father, Gavin Hadden III, was a lifelong construction executive, building things his entire life—schools, hospitals, big projects. When he retired to Kennebunkport, Maine, he kept busy building things, not out of steel and concrete but out of butter and flour. He traded in his hard hat for an apron, and his workshop was the kitchen. In the morning he'd make cakes and pies and scones, then take them to share with his pals at the golf club. He was a great golfer and a pretty good baker.

One morning Gavin's mom woke up to the whole house smelling like a batch of his chocolate chip cookies. She went downstairs to the kitchen, but the oven was off. There was nobody there; her husband had died the year before.

But as she stood there, she could smell his cookies—it was so real, so vivid.

She knows it was a sign from him. I think she's right.

The most humbling part of the process of writing this cookbook has been listening to the really personal stories of people who have strong feelings sparked by food. These recipes aren't just a combination of ingredients stirred in a bowl and baked until done. There's another dimension to them that we often don't realize, there's a sentimentality, a poignancy, a super-strong emotion you get when you smell or see a food from your past—or, as a fighter pilot in Iraq, simply remember something sitting on a plate at home in your kitchen. Something that's waiting for you.

Italian-born Elena Coscia was the mother of our next-door neighbor, Laura. We went to a dozen family festivities and she always brought the cake. Birthday, anniversary, graduation, confirmation, Super Bowl—you name the holiday and you could take it to the bank that there would be a yellow lemon cake there. She made that cake hundreds, maybe thousands, of times. It was expected that if Elena was invited, she'd be bringing that cake.

"Oh, you're the lemon cake lady," I heard people who didn't know her say. "I gotta get your recipe!" *Everybody* wanted it.

Living across the street from them for twenty years, I've seen with my own eyes the family that Elena and her husband, Frank, raised. Wonderful, warm, always inviting us into their lives to share a celebration. The grandkids loved their grandma, as did her children and all who knew her. She was a permanent fixture in their lives, and ours.

And then she died.

She'd not been in good health for a while, but she had been so active and full of life the last time we saw her; she had just brought that lemon cake to her grandson Joseph's backyard graduation party.

The day Elena died, as the family gathered to plan the funeral, somebody realized that this was the first time anybody could remember that they

Sally with our version of Elena's Lemon Cake.

were all together and there was no lemon cake.

Laura's sister, Ann, said, "I've got to go to Staples."

Two days later at the funeral, next to the mass cards commemorating Elena's life, the family placed a stack of freshly printed 4 x 6 cards bearing something you don't see at many funerals: a recipe.

Elena's Lemon Cake, with exact instructions in the voice of the beloved baker.

That cake, which had been her calling card for so many years, will be baked and shared and loved thousands more times in the future. It was the ultimate tribute from a family that will never forget.

When we first made the cake at our house after she passed, I called Laura with a question about the icing. She asked, "Could you take a picture of it?"

I sent a snapshot to her and she wrote back, "Looks just like it's supposed to look."

It dawned on me after I hung up that I couldn't just email her a picture. Five minutes later I was knocking on her door, holding a cake that was missing three pieces.

I couldn't keep it. It wasn't our cake; it was her mom's.

The legacy of the lemon cake.

I bet you're thinking right now, *What will my family remember me for? What's my lemon cake?*

The good news is, you have a lifetime to figure that out.

My grandma Sharp had been a cook all her life, and wisely taught her daughters, Linda and JoAnne, how to make all of the foods they grew up with and would need to feed a family. My mom and her sister then handed those recipes down to the next generation, my generation. That's how I learned to cook.

In 1978, when I walked into Grandma's house at 808 North Minnesota Street in Algona, Iowa, on the day of her funeral, my mom asked me if there was anything I wanted to take to remind me of Grandma.

"Yes."

I looked around and then I found them, sitting there all alone on her stove, just where she had left them: her salt and pepper shakers. She was always tasting something and adding a little of this or a lot of that, and it always made dinner perfect.

The shakers are simple pine, with chickens hand-painted on the sides. They probably cost a dollar when she bought them, but to me they are priceless. I still have them. I've never washed them, so they have her fingerprints on them, and mine.

If there's one thing we hope you've learned from this book, and in particular from the last few stories about people who have passed from our

Grandma bought these for a dollar; they're now priceless to us.

lives, it's that they live on in us through their recipes . . . Gavin's dad's cookies, Elena's lemon cake, my mom's gravy.

You may think making those special eggs for your kids on Sunday morning is no big deal, but one day those kids will be grown and gone, and if they ever have a flashback and have a yearning for your special eggs, I hope you showed them how to make them, so they can enjoy them, and if you're lucky, share them with their children.

The legacy of your special eggs.

When you think about it, a family's history can be really fragile, with the significant stories we hope somebody in the next generation will remember and pass on, the shoebox full of black-and-white pictures of people whose names will be forgotten if we don't write them down, and the recipes that made home, home.

So how do you keep those memories alive? You could go to Staples and print up your lemon cake recipe, or do something this simple: Write down a list of your favorite family recipes, and next time you make them, take some pictures with your phone. Then, when you have a couple dozen, make a photo book online, and Walgreens or Shutterfly or Apple will print it and send it to your house. It's something you can be proud of, because it's not just directions for how to make Aunt Mary's pot roast, it's really about Aunt Mary, and you, and your family, and the meals that make your memories.

That book will become an heirloom, and everybody in your family will want a copy.

It took us about a year to create our version, and you're holding it—thank you.

Kathy and I want to be remembered as good cooks, but it's more important for us to be great parents who tried to do the right things and gave our children the tools to be happy and successful. With this book, they'll also now have a pretty good idea how to make the foods they, and we, grew up with and loved.

Just know that two of my favorite childhood recollections, salmon patties and creamed peas on toast, are not in this cookbook. They may have given me fond food flashbacks to the 1960s, but when I made the salmon patties and creamed peas

this year for my family, exactly as my mom made them, they were downright gross. They had their moment, but did not survive the test of time; they'd now qualify for Buzzfeed's Top 10 Foods from My Childhood That Now Make Me Queasy.

Time marches on and tastes change, but recipes can last forever.

Case in point; the oldest known written recipe is from 1800 BC, and it's for beer. Just imagine if that guy hadn't written down his earth-changing discovery. What would you buy to thank a hero at a bar if there was no beer? A Bellini? Get real. . . .

Thankfully, we have beer today because somebody wrote down a recipe a long time ago, giving Budweiser something to do aside from raising the world's coolest big horses.

Write down your recipes; they can last this lifetime and many more.

And with that we thank you for reading our cookbook. We wish you the very best as you try your hand at these recipes, which have brought much happiness to our family and friends and now, we hope, yours.

So many memories, so little thyme.

Sincerely,

Steve & Kathy Doocy

HAMBURGER COOKIES

• M A K E S   4 0   " H A M B U R G E R S " •

Kathy saw these hamburger cookies at a school event and asked the neighbor who'd made them for a copy of the recipe. Her answer was not what Kathy expected.

"I'll give it to you, but you can't make it until my kids are out of this elementary school."

Okay, clearly she wanted to be known for those cookies. But once her kids were in middle school, Kathy got the green light and the cookie torch was passed.

The finished cookies are so simple, but they look so precious and perfect that when I took a batch to work not long ago, one of my coworkers said, "That's a cookie? It looks like something Tiffany's would sell."

1 cup sweetened shredded coconut (for the lettuce)
Green food coloring
One 16-ounce carton ready-to-spread vanilla frosting (for the ketchup and mayo)
Red food coloring
80 Nilla wafers (for the buns)
40 Keebler Grasshopper cookies (for the burger)

1. In a zip-top bag, combine the coconut and a few drops of green food coloring. Close the bag and shake it around until the coconut is all green, like lettuce.

2. Divide the frosting between two small bowls. In one, mix in red food coloring until the frosting is the color of ketchup. The other bowl of frosting will be the mayo.

3. For each hamburger cookie, use 2 Nilla wafers for a top and bottom bun. Spoon about 1 teaspoon of the "mayo" onto the center of the flat side of a wafer. Place a "burger" (Grasshopper cookie) on the frosting, then add about 1 teaspoon of the "ketchup" and a big pinch of the green coconut "lettuce." Place the second Nilla wafer on top and gently squeeze the "burger" to help fuse it together. Repeat to make the rest of the burgers.

4. Place each burger in a cupcake liner and let them rest 20 minutes to set.

NUTELLA HANDHELD PIES

When I worked at NBC, we lived on the Upper East Side of Manhattan, which at that time was not very family friendly. There were few high chairs in restaurants, and Kathy's double stroller was such an oddity that when she'd go grocery shopping at the Food Emporium, a manager would walk behind her to make sure she wasn't shoplifting. Once three crooks blocked her into a corner and she was mugged at the salad bar.

"So much for healthy eating," she told the cop who wrote her police report.

The highlight of the neighborhood was a cute little bakery on the corner of 57th Street that had the most beautiful baked goods. After we moved to New Jersey we continued to use the sweets they had in their window as our inspiration for all sorts of delights, including this one that the kids asked us to make for them. It's a combination of Nutella and crust—the best part of a pie. Think of it as the world's best Pop-Tart.

To make these more festive, use a seasonal cookie cutter, such as a heart around Valentine's Day or a Christmas tree at the closing of the year.

2 store-bought pie crusts
7 teaspoons Nutella
½ cup mini marshmallows
Fig jam
Egg wash: 1 egg whisked with 1 tablespoon
    water

DRIZZLE
2 tablespoons butter, at room temperature
¼ cup Nutella
⅓ cup powdered sugar
Milk, as needed

1. Preheat the oven to 375°F.

2. On parchment paper, unroll one pie crust. Use a 3½-inch biscuit cutter to cut 7 rounds from the dough. You can combine the scraps and then roll them out with a rolling pin to make a few bonus pieces. Lay the rounds on an ungreased baking sheet.

3. Place 1 teaspoon Nutella in the center of each round and smooth it out to within ¾ inch of the edge. Place 1 or 2 mini marshmallows in the center; this will give the pie a little height during baking.

4. Roll out the second pie crust and cut 7 more rounds. Place 1 teaspoon of fig jam on each and spread out to ¾ inch from the edge.

5. Run a moistened finger around the edge of each Nutella round to help seal the pies. Invert a jelly round over each Nutella round and press the edges with your finger to seal them (or use a fork to crimp the edges). Poke a couple steam holes in the top of each pie.

6. Brush the top of each pie with egg wash.

7. Bake until perfectly golden, 13 to 15 minutes. Set the pies on a wire rack to cool.

8. While the pies are cooling, make the drizzle: In a medium bowl, combine the butter, Nutella, and powdered sugar and stir until smooth. If the mixture is a bit dry, add a tiny bit of milk to make it drizzleable. Place it in a pastry bag (or in a zip-top bag with the corner snipped off).

9. When the pies are cool, drizzle them with patterns of your choosing. Let the pies rest while the drizzle sets, then call the kids.

I ♥ BIG APPLE PIE

We love pie.

Growing up in Southern California, Kathy's family would make frequent trips to a place called Du-par's of Encino to pick a pie for dessert. So many to choose from, but Kathy loved apple the most. Now we live outside New York, the Big Apple, but just to be troublemakers, we don't make *big* apple pies; we make these *little* apple hand pies, which are just enough for anybody with a sweet tooth.

PIES
One 13.2-ounce package Wewalka Puff
   Pastry dough
½ cup apple pie filling
Ground cinnamon, for dusting
4 tablespoons (½ stick) butter, melted

ICING
¼ cup powdered sugar
½ tablespoon butter, at room temperature
1 teaspoon milk

1. Preheat the oven to 400°F.

2. To make the pies: Roll out both pieces of puff pastry dough (Wewalka comes with its own parchment paper). Use a 3-inch heart-shaped cookie cutter to cut out as many pieces as you can (you'll probably get between 8 and 10 pieces per puff pastry sheet). If you end up with an odd number, combine the dough scraps and cut out one more piece.

3. Place the apple pie filling in a small bowl. Remove the apple pieces and cut them into a dice smaller than ½ inch, then return them to the filling and stir them back in.

4. Place half of the hearts on an ungreased baking sheet, leaving a couple inches between them. Drop a spoonful of the apple mixture onto the middle of each heart. Experiment with how much you can use; it will be between a teaspoon and a tablespoon. Leave about ¾ inch of bare space around the edges. Sprinkle a dusting of ground cinnamon over the apple mixture, then paint the pastry edges with melted butter.

5. Set a top pastry heart on each bottom heart and use a fork to crimp the edges. Brush the hearts with melted butter.

6. Bake until the pies are golden and delicious, 15 to 18 minutes. Let the pies cool on a wire rack.

7. To make the icing: In a medium bowl, combine the powdered sugar, butter, and milk and stir until smooth. Add a little more sugar if it's too thin. Immediately place the icing in a pastry bag (or zip-top bag with a small corner snipped off) and drizzle it over the apple hearts in patterns of your choosing (zigzags always look great). Or draw a # with the icing and your kids will Instagram them for sure. Hashtag heart pies trending!

LEMON MERINGUE PIE

My mother was famous for her mile-high meringue pies. I believe she learned how to make them from her mother, who was a cook at a diner on the north side of Algona, Iowa, called Frank & Fm's and later renamed The Chrome, because it had—as you'd imagine—a lot of chrome.

My aunt Linda told me that Grandma loved to bake with lard, and it was the secret to her super-flaky pie crusts. Of course if we cooked with lard today, my cardiologist would come to our house and make a citizen's arrest.

I remember as a little boy going to Grandma's diner and seeing the meringues soaring like clouds floating off the pie. I was so proud that my grandma made all those pies. To me, she was the greatest chef in the world.

I also loved it there because I ate for free.

PIE AND FILLING
1 store-bought pie crust
One 2.75-ounce box My*T*Fine lemon
    pudding and pie filling
½ cup sugar
2 large egg yolks

MERINGUE TOPPING
4 large egg whites
½ teaspoon cream of tartar
Dash of salt
½ teaspoon pure vanilla extract
½ cup sugar

1. Position a rack in the center of the oven and preheat the oven to 450°F.

2. To make the pie and filling: Unroll the crust and place in a 9-inch pie pan. Poke the bottom with a fork a couple times. Bake the empty pie shell until golden, about 10 minutes. Set aside to cool. Leave the oven on, but reduce the temperature to 350°F.

3. Grandma was a professional, and she used this pie filling, so it must be good. In a saucepan, combine the contents of the pie filling mix, the sugar, and ¼ cup water. Stir in the egg yolks and 2 cups water. Set the pan over medium heat and cook, stirring constantly, until it eventually bubbles and boils. Remove from the heat, let it cool 5 minutes, and stir twice. Scoop the lemon filling into the cooled pie crust and spread it out evenly.

4. To make the meringue topping: In a bowl, with an electric mixer, beat the egg whites, cream of tartar, salt, and vanilla on medium speed until it gets frothy. Beat on high speed, slowly adding the sugar until the meringue is stiff and shiny. When you think it's ready, beat another 30 seconds.

5. Use a spatula to spread the meringue over the lemon filling (we love to make it unbelievably high, creating decorative peaks and swirls). Bake until the meringue swirls start turning golden brown, about 10 minutes.

6. Cool completely, refrigerate, and serve.

GWEN'S FLOURLESS CHOCOLATE CAKE

·MAKES ONE 9-INCH CAKE·

Kathy's brother-in-law Rob and his wife, Gwen, are the most athletic members of our family. Longtime California and Colorado residents, they introduced us to surfing, golf, and rock climbing. They also are healthy eaters and can probably tell you their current LDL and HDL cholesterol levels within 5 mg. I don't exactly know my current HDL or LDL, but I do know my UPS guy's name and worry about him when he still wears his brown shorts in the winter.

This is Rob and Gwen and their son Dane's happy dessert. Gwen told me her happy factor is baking a cake for people she loves . . . and isn't that why we all do it?

Whenever we make this cake here in New Jersey, we imagine we're at their beach house in Del Mar, looking out at the Pacific, laughing about the old days and waiting for the green flash as the sun goes down and officially signals it's time to have another glass of California Chardonnay, because we're on vacation, eating chocolate cake!

2 sticks (½ pound) butter, plus more for the pan
18 ounces Ghirardelli semisweet chocolate chips
Dash of salt
6 large eggs
Whipped cream or powdered sugar and fresh berries (raspberries, strawberries, blueberries), for serving

1. Preheat the oven to 325°F.
2. Butter a 9-inch springform pan, cover the bottom with a round of parchment paper cut to fit it, and butter the paper. Wrap doubled foil around the outside of the pan to make it watertight. Place the prepared pan in a large roasting pan and set aside.
3. In a double boiler, melt the chocolate chips and 2 sticks butter. Add the salt, give a stir until smooth, and set aside to cool.
4. Bring a teakettle or a medium saucepan of water to a boil over high heat.
5. In a large bowl, with an electric mixer, whip the eggs until fluffy. Fold the eggs into the cooled chocolate mixture. Pour the mixture into the prepared cake pan.
6. Pull out the oven rack and set the roasting pan on the rack. Carefully pour boiling water into the roasting pan so that it goes about halfway up the sides of the springform pan.
7. Bake the cake until it has risen slightly and the edges are starting to set but the center still looks soft or wet, about 45 minutes.
8. Remove the springform pan from the water and place it on a cooling rack. Remove the foil from the pan and set the pan in the fridge to chill.
9. Remove the cake from the fridge about 20 minutes before serving. Unlatch the side from the springform pan, invert the cake onto a plate, remove the pan bottom and parchment paper, and re-invert the cake onto a serving dish.
10. We love to serve the cake with whipped cream . . . and a glass of wine. Or dust with powdered sugar and serve with fresh berries. It's so rich that you'll have leftovers—refrigerate them!

DR. OZ'S GERMAN CHOCOLATE CAKE

·MAKES ONE 8-INCH LAYER CAKE·

When I asked America's most famous cardiologist for his favorite happy food, I figured it would be something with a bale of kale or made with matcha, so I was shocked when he said, "German chocolate cake!"

The good doctor's wife, Lisa, knows that's right, and told me, "The only thing Mehmet asks for on his birthday is this ultradecadent chocolate cake. Oh, don't look so shocked! He just eats one piece, and it's only once a year. The first time I made it for him was over thirty years ago with my friend Marilyn. The recipe has evolved from her classic version to a darker chocolate cake, but it's still got that sticky-sweet-gooey coconut icing."

Of course Lisa is a world-famous cookbook author herself, so I wouldn't expect this to be anything but fantastic; and as it turns out, Kathy and I agree that *this is the best cake we have ever made!*

GERMAN CHOCOLATE CAKE
1 cup boiling water
¾ cup unsweetened cocoa powder
⅔ cup plain Greek yogurt
⅔ cup whole milk
½ teaspoon cider vinegar
10 tablespoons (1¼ sticks) unsalted butter, at room temperature, plus more for the pans
1¾ cups unbleached all-purpose flour, plus more for the pans
2 cups organic sugar
3 large eggs, at room temperature
1 teaspoon pure vanilla extract
1½ teaspoons baking soda
¼ teaspoon fine sea salt

COCONUT-PECAN ICING
8 tablespoons (1 stick) unsalted butter, cut into tablespoons
Two 14-ounce cans non-GMO condensed milk
6 large egg yolks
2 cups unsweetened shredded coconut
2 cups coarsely chopped walnuts or pecans (8 ounces)
2 teaspoons pure vanilla extract
⅛ teaspoon fine sea salt

1. To make the German chocolate cake: In a medium bowl, whisk together the boiling water and cocoa to dissolve the cocoa. Refrigerate, whisking often, until the mixture has cooled completely.

2. In a glass measuring cup, whisk together the yogurt, milk, and vinegar. Set aside at room temperature while the cocoa mixture is cooling.

3. Position a rack in the center of the oven and preheat the oven to 350°F. Lightly butter two 8-inch round cake pans and line the bottoms with wax or parchment paper. Dust the sides of the pan with flour and tap out the excess.

4. In a bowl, with an electric mixer, beat the butter on high speed until creamy, about 1 minute. Gradually beat in the sugar and continue mixing, scraping down the side of the bowl as needed, until the mixture is light in color and texture, about 2 minutes. One at a time, beat in the eggs, beating well after each addition, followed by the vanilla. With the mixer on low speed, beat in the cooled cocoa mixture.

5. In a separate bowl, whisk together the flour, baking soda, and salt, being sure the baking soda is pulverized. With the mixer on low speed, alternately add the flour mixture and the yogurt mixture to the butter mixture, beginning and ending with the flour, mixing just until combined after each addition. Scrape the batter into the cake pans and smooth the tops.

6. Bake until a wooden toothpick inserted into the center of the cakes comes out clean, about 35 minutes. Let the cakes cool in the pans on a wire cooling rack for 10 minutes. Run a knife around the inside edge of each pan. Invert the pans onto the rack to unmold the cakes. Flip the cakes, right side up, and let cool completely.

7. To make the coconut-pecan icing: In a medium, heavy-bottomed saucepan, melt the butter over medium heat. Stir in the condensed milk and cook, stirring often, until the mixture is simmering.

8. In a medium bowl, whisk the egg yolks together. Gradually beat in about 1 cup of the hot condensed milk mixture, and pour this back into the saucepan. Cook, stirring constantly, until the mixture returns to a simmer and thickens, about 10 minutes. Transfer the mixture to a large bowl. Stir in the coconut, walnuts, vanilla, and salt. Let the icing cool for a few minutes until it is thick enough to spread.

9. Place a cake layer, flat side facing up, on a serving plate. Spread it with about ¾ cup of the icing. Top with the second cake layer, flat side down. Spread the top, and then the sides, with the remaining icing. Let the icing cool completely. The cake can be stored at room temperature for up to 1 day. You can put it in the fridge or invite some friends over. Truthfully, there's never much left. Slice and serve.

WALNUT-Y THUMBPRINT COOKIES

My great-grandma would always have a plate of these cookies on her sideboard in the dining room for Sunday lunches. She was 100 percent Swedish, and when she came over on the boat to America she surely had sewn this recipe into the lining of her coat in case there was trouble at sea.

When our fourth-grade daughter Mary was assigned Sweden as a geography project, Kathy suggested that she pass out some Swedish cookies, so I suggested my great-grandma's recipe. Mary wanted to know what her name was in Swedish, so they Googled "Swedish Mary," and up popped a shocking array of pictures. I say shocking because Sweden is famous for its cold weather, and these Swedish Marys were wearing very few clothes.

Kathy immediately hit the *off* button, and they proceeded to bake these cookies in shocked silence.

By the way, the Swedish translation of Mary Is "Mary."

1½ sticks (6 ounces) butter, at room temperature, plus more for the baking sheets
¾ cup butter-flavored Crisco
1 cup sugar
3 large eggs, separated
1 teaspoon pure vanilla extract
½ teaspoon salt
3 cups flour
2 cups finely chopped walnuts
About ½ cup of your favorite jam (strawberry, apricot, raspberry)

1. Preheat the oven to 375°F. Grease 2 full-size baking sheets.

2. In a bowl, with an electric mixer, cream together the butter, Crisco, and sugar. Add the egg yolks, vanilla, and salt and slowly mix in the flour until smooth. Wrap the dough in plastic and refrigerate for at least 20 minutes.

3. Meanwhile, in a separate bowl, with the mixer, whip the egg whites until frothy. Place the nuts in a shallow bowl.

4. When ready to bake, form the dough into compact 1-inch balls. Dip each into the egg whites, then roll in the nuts. Place the balls on a the prepared baking sheets, spacing them 2 inches apart. With your finger, press a thumbprint dent into the center of each ball.

5. Bake the cookies, until they inflate a bit, 10 to 15 minutes.

6. Pull the cookies out of the oven (leave the oven on) and if necessary, make the thumbprint dents a bit deeper; use the back side of a 1-teaspoon measuring spoon. Spoon about ½ teaspoon jam into each thumbprint. Return to the oven and bake until lightly browned, 7 to 8 minutes.

7. Transfer the cookies to a cooling rack or wax paper. They will still be a little soft, so be careful!

NUTELLA S'MORES

·MAKES 6 TO 8 SERVINGS·

There is no happier taste of summer nights than s'mores. But let's be honest, how often do you have a roaring campfire in your backyard—on purpose?

After many s'mores-eating summers at Sea Island in Georgia and Palmetto Bluff in South Carolina, our daughter Sally invented these. She loved the taste of s'mores but hated standing in the downdraft of a big, smoky fire—that smell clings to your clothes until you donate them to Goodwill.

This recipe requires no campfire, just an oven, and there are no long sticks to poke an eye out. And because s'mores are by design gooey and *very* messy, Sally made these to be eaten with a spoon.

They're quick and easy and taste like the original, but rather than a Hershey's bar, they use Nutella!

1 cup Nutella, or more as desired
Store-bought graham cracker pie crust (or Oreo crust, your choice)
One 16-ounce bag large marshmallows

1. Preheat the oven to 450°F.

2. Spread the Nutella in the pie crust. It should be at least ½ inch deep; if not, add a little more. Arrange the marshmallows on the Nutella.

3. Bake until the marshmallows are golden brown, 5 to 7 minutes.

4. Remove smores from the oven, let sit a few minutes, then give everybody a spoon and dig in!

BROWNIE WAFFLES

When the going gets tough . . . the tough go shopping.

When we remodeled our kitchen to get fancy new stainless steel appliances, which Kathy referred to as *kitchen jewelry*, we were without an oven and stove for a month. We loved eating nonstop takeout for about two weeks, then we wanted dinner made our way. We got very creative with the microwave, but you can't nuke everything; some things need that crunch that you just can't get with the microwave. So we went shopping online and bought a new waffle iron.

Some of our waffle iron experiments included waffled polenta (so-so), waffle chocolate chip cookies (pretty good), and mashed potatoes with cheese (surprisingly good). But our favorite was the waffle brownie. The genius of these is that when you get a taste for baked brownies, you don't have to wait 45 minutes for them to bake—once they're in the iron they're done in 5 minutes. Which is microwave-fast!

Why did we spend thousands on a fancy new oven when all we really needed was a $25 Oster waffle iron off Amazon?

1 box brownie mix
Oil and/or egg as required by the mix, plus
    1 extra egg
Cooking spray

OPTIONAL TOPPINGS
Whipped cream
Chocolate syrup
Caramel syrup
Rainbow sprinkles
Milk chocolate flakes
Ice cream

1. Preheat a waffle iron to medium heat.

2. Prepare the brownie batter according to the box directions and stir in an extra egg. Blend until smooth.

3. Coat the top and bottom plates of the waffle iron with cooking spray. Pour about ½ cup brownie batter onto the waffle maker for a three-quarter-size brownie, or more if you want a full-size brownie. See what works best in your waffle iron.

4. Close the lid and cook for 5 or 6 minutes. Turn off the iron, open the lid, but don't immediately remove the waffle; it needs to sit and firm up for a couple minutes. Gently lift the edges about ½ inch on all sides with a fork to make sure it's not stuck anywhere, then place a plate on top of the waffle and invert the iron. The brownie will fall onto the plate. Let it sit a minute, then decorate, as desired.

5. Plenty of batter left—repeat the process and make more!

HASSELBACK BAKED APPLE

We first noticed the Hasselbacking of America's potatoes as chefs were turning a lonely spud into a work of art. It's easy to Hasselback potatoes, but we started doing it with apples, because the kids pick a lot of them at nearby orchards and we need something to do with them.

Because making these does involve focusing on small cuts with a big knife, may I suggest that you hold off on that big glass of wine you've been looking forward to all day? That is, unless you enjoy the ER and have met your deductible for the year.

Cooking spray
2 tablespoons light brown sugar
4 tablespoons (½ stick) butter, melted
1 teaspoon apple pie spice
¼ cup pure maple syrup, plus more as needed
2 Honeycrisp apples, cored, peeled, and halved through the core
¼ cup very finely chopped walnut halves
Vanilla ice cream or whipped cream, for serving

1. Preheat the oven to 400°F. Coat a medium baking dish with cooking spray.
2. In a small bowl, combine the brown sugar, melted butter, apple pie spice, and maple syrup. Set aside.

3. Place an apple half cut side down on a cutting board and place a wooden spoon on each side, parallel with the core, so you won't cut all the way through the apple. Carefully slice the apple crosswise making cuts ⅛ inch apart. Repeat with the rest of the apple halves.
4. Place the apples flat side down in the prepared baking dish. Brush about half the maple syrup mixture between the slices by gently fanning the slices open. Cover with foil and bake for 20 minutes.
5. Meanwhile, stir the walnuts into the remaining maple syrup mixture. If it has firmed up, microwave it for 15 seconds, then give a stir. If it's still too firm, add about 1 tablespoon maple syrup.
6. Uncover the apples and top with the walnut mixture, pushing the walnuts down between the slices. Bake uncovered for 10 minutes more.
7. Let the apples cool a bit, then serve with ice cream or whipped cream or whatever you put on apple pie.

4-H CLUB CHOCOLATE SHEET CAKE

When I was growing up in Kansas, I was the president of the Future Farmers of America for Clay Center Community High School. I knew I wasn't going to be a farmer, but I needed a fallback career in case my dream job of newspaper reporter didn't pan out, so I took agriculture classes to learn how to weld. I still know how to do it, and I'm patiently waiting for Neil Cavuto to ask me to come into his office and arc-weld that missing wheel back onto his desk chair.

My entire family also belonged to the Industry Kansas 4-H Club. My parents were local leaders and my sisters and I were members until I went to high school. I raised pigs and rabbits as livestock projects and learned photography and public speaking, two things that helped get me where I am today. We'd sing carols at the old folks' home every Christmas season, theoretically to make them feel good, but actually it made us all feel needed and loved.

My dad was a real artist, and our club won all sorts of awards for creative displays, and my mom was a good cook; she taught me how to bake and showed me the way around the kitchen, which culminated in me winning a blue ribbon at the Kansas State Fair for chocolate chip cookies. I never told anybody this, but that recipe was not handed down from my family. It came from the back of the yellow Nestlé Toll House semi-sweet chocolate chip bag.

This recipe is for a cake my mom baked for every 4-H meeting, box social, or community fundraiser. Every family on Rural Route 1 in Clay County, Kansas, used essentially this same recipe. Sometimes five families would bring the same cake, and there were never any leftovers.

Butter, for the baking sheet
Flour, for the baking sheet

CAKE
1¾ cups sugar
½ cup Crisco
6 tablespoons unsweetened cocoa powder
¼ teaspoon salt
1 teaspoon baking soda
1 teaspoon bourbon vanilla extract or regular pure vanilla extract
1 cup cold water
2 cups flour
3 large egg whites

FROSTING
8 tablespoons (1 stick) butter
¼ cup unsweetened cocoa powder
¼ cup + 2 tablespoons fat-free half-and-half (or milk)
¼ teaspoon salt
1 pound powdered sugar
1 teaspoon bourbon vanilla extract or regular pure vanilla extract
½ cup chopped walnut halves

Vanilla ice cream, for serving

1. Preheat the oven to 325°F convection (or 350°F standard). Grease and flour a 12 x 17-inch rimmed baking sheet

2. To make the cake: In a bowl, with an electric mixer, beat the sugar and Crisco on low speed until it's evenly grainy. Slowly add the remaining ingredients in order as the mixer runs. When the batter is very smooth, pour it into the prepared pan.

3. Bake until a toothpick inserted into the center comes out clean, 30 to 35 minutes.

4. Meanwhile, make the frosting: In a medium saucepan, combine the butter, cocoa, and half-and-half and stir over medium heat until the butter is melted and the mixture is smooth. Remove from the heat.

5. Using the mixer again, blend the salt and powdered sugar on low speed. Pour in the butter/cocoa mixture and vanilla and mix until perfectly uniform.

6. While the cake is still warm, use a spatula to spread the frosting over the cake, making the surface as smooth as you can. The heat will smooth out the rest. Sprinkle the walnuts evenly over the frosting and wait for it to set up, then cut the cake into squares.

7. Serve warm and with vanilla ice cream.

GRANITA DI CAFFÈ

Across the street from the Pantheon in Rome is one of the most famous coffee shops in the world, La Casa del Caffè Tazza d'Oro. America runs on Dunkin', and Rome apparently runs on d'Oro.

We were tourists one very hot day and because we didn't speak Italian and the order taker didn't speak English, we relied upon our son, Peter, to order the coffee drinks, because he'd taken two years of high school Italian. As he was ordering, a troubled look came over the face of the barista. (I later looked up in our translation book what Peter was saying, and Peter sounded like he was trying to order a boiled tractor.)

So we did the natural tourist thing—after the cashier said, "No, no, no!" we went to plan B and pointed at what everybody else was having: the *granita di caffè* that they were famous for creating. It was terrific. But because of the language difference we could not ask them how they made it—I'm sure they had a granita machine—so when we got home we created our own version that is pretty simple and ultimately much more refreshing than a boiled tractor.

½ cup sugar
2 cups very strong coffee, hot
Reddi-wip or other canned whipped cream
Piece of dark chocolate

1. In a medium bowl, dissolve the sugar in the hot coffee. Next, you have two different ways to make the ice coffee crystals. The *fastest,* is to pour the coffee into ice cube trays and carefully place them in freezer. Once frozen solid, place the cubes in a large doubled zip-top bag, squeeze out any extra air, and using a wooden rolling pin, gently crush the cubes. Don't pulverize them too much, grainy is better. Another way to make *fluffier* ice crystals (but it takes more elbow grease) is to freeze the coffee in a cake pan. Once the coffee is frozen solid, remove the pan from the freezer and, using a spoon or fork, scrape the surface of the coffee back and forth creating frozen crystals. Once you've done the entire pan, level the surface with your spoon or fork and put the pan back in the freezer. After at least 90 minutes, repeat the scraping process, creating a well-worked pile of frozen flakes.

2. Now let's layer it up. For each serving, in a small clear serving cup, squirt a little whipped cream into the bottom, level it out, then spoon in a few tablespoons of the frozen granita to make a layer about as thick as the whipped cream. Repeat the layers, then top with a nice big squirt of whipped cream. Shave some dark chocolate on the top, grab a spoon, and enjoy! If serving for breakfast, have a nice pastry ready.

3. *"Quel trattore bollito è delizioso!"*

KATHY'S FAMOUS SUGAR COOKIES

For the last thirty-some years, whenever we went anywhere for a visit, Kathy would bake a couple dozen of these cookies, put them on a pretty plate, wrap them in cellophane, tie a bow around the top, and take them as a hostess gift. It's easier to just bring a bottle of wine, but not that many people spend two hours of their life making something from scratch.

We've been invited to some of the most fantastic New York City parties, where the hosts spend thousands of dollars catering, and still Kathy takes her cookies, which are always happily accepted and set in a prominent place on the dessert table, next to the fancy stuff from Zabar's or Balducci's. And it's always easy to get our plate back at the end of the night, because the plate is always empty.

Our kids ask for these every time they come home for a visit. The cookies hold fond memories for them because they helped Kathy bake them for years. In fact, if you go into our kitchen right now you'll see sugar sprinkles from these cookies in the cracks of our antique pine farm table.

2 sticks (½ pound) butter, at room temperature
1 large egg
1 teaspoon baking soda
2 teaspoons fresh lemon juice
1½ teaspoons pure vanilla extract
1½ teaspoons almond extract
1⅓ cups powdered sugar
2⅔ cups flour
Colored sugar sprinkles

1. In a bowl, with an electric mixer, cream together the butter, egg, baking soda, lemon juice, vanilla, almond extract, and powdered sugar. Slowly add the flour and mix until it's thoroughly blended.

2. Divide the dough in two parts, cover them in plastic wrap, and then press them out flat, so the dough will be easier to roll out later. Chill in the fridge at least 2 hours.

3. Preheat the oven to 375°F. On lightly floured parchment paper, press the dough out as flat as you can with your hands. Dust the top of the dough with flour and place another piece of parchment paper on top. Using a rolling pin, roll out the dough to about ¼ inch thick.

4. Cut out the cookies with cookie cutters. Carefully lay the cookies 1 inch apart on an ungreased baking sheet. Ball up the dough scraps, lightly flour and reroll to make more.

5. Now it's time to decorate with colored sprinkles. Kathy likes to simply shake a single color of the sugar over each cookie as you can see in the photograph. But she does use several different colors with every batch.

6. Bake on the center rack until edges turn slightly golden, 8 to 10 minutes. Let cool. Eat one. Maybe two . . .

MARY'S EASY APPLE GALETTE

·MAKES 6 SERVINGS·

When my mom would make an apple pie crust from scratch, she'd always have some extra cut-up dough corners, and she'd combine them into a single piece of dough, roll it out, cut it into long strips, sprinkle on sugar and cinnamon, and bake the strips until they were browned. The pie itself would have to wait for Dad to come home, but these she'd serve hot out of the oven. My sister Jenny makes them for her kids and calls it Grandma's toast.

You know the expression, easy as pie? This apple galette is easier than pie. No fluting, no crimping, no pie pan—it's free-form and fabulous.

Our daughter Mary, who is just learning to bake on her own, brought home this rustic recipe Basically, if you can fold a flap of dough over some apples, this will be your pie pièce de résistance.

    ¼ cup packed light brown sugar
    1 teaspoon apple pie spice
    1 store-bought pie crust
    2 Granny Smith apples
    2 tablespoons fresh lemon juice
    1 tablespoon butter, cut into small pieces
    3 tablespoons chopped walnuts or pecans
    1 large egg
    1 tablespoon heavy cream
    Vanilla ice cream or whipped cream, for
       serving

1. Position a rack in the center of the oven and preheat the oven to 400°F.

2. In a small bowl, combine the brown sugar and apple pie spice.

3. Unroll the pie crust onto parchment paper or a silicone baking sheet set on a large baking sheet.

4. Peel and core the apples and slice them into thin half-moons. In a large bowl, combine the apples and lemon juice and mix gently (this keeps the apples from browning). Sprinkle the brown sugar mixture over the apples and mix lightly to coat.

5. Arrange the apples on the dough in a decorative overlapping pattern, leaving a couple inches of the dough free around the edges. Dot the apples with the butter and toss on the nuts. Fold the dough edges in over the apples, pleating them closed in a rustic fashion, leaving most of the apples uncovered in the middle.

6. In a small bowl, whisk the egg and cream. Brush this egg wash on the exposed dough.

7. Bake until the apples are bubbling and the crust is deep golden, 50 to 60 minutes.

8. Slice (a pizza cutter works great!) and serve with vanilla ice cream or whipped cream.

BASEBALL BLUEBERRY BUCKLE

· MAKES 12 SERVINGS ·

Our son, Peter, played baseball in high school. Kathy is the only parent I know who can say she went not only to every game but also to every practice. So it's an understatement to say we spent a lot of time in the bleachers, which is a very social place to be. Different parents would bring a variety of snacks to the events, and it would help pass the time as we waited for our team's pitcher to strike out that last kid from Fairlawn, so we could finally go home and have a glass of Concha y Toro from Costco.

One mom had just returned from New England and was such a fan of the blueberry buckle she had had up there that she baked a big pan of it and brought it to the game. There was supposed to be some left over for the boys after the game . . . sorry, kids. Kathy asked for the recipe and at the next game, the other mom had it copied onto an index card. We still have it in our collection.

Cooking spray

TOPPING
½ cup sugar
⅓ cup flour
½ teaspoon ground cinnamon
4 tablespoons (½ stick) butter, at room temperature

BATTER
2 cups flour
¾ cup sugar

2½ teaspoons baking powder
¾ teaspoon salt
4 tablespoons (½ stick) butter, at room temperature
1 large egg
¾ cup milk
2 cups blueberries

Vanilla ice cream or whipped cream, for serving

1. Position a rack in the center of the oven and preheat the oven to 375°F. Coat a 9 x 9-inch baking pan with cooking spray.
2. To make the topping: In a medium bowl, combine the topping ingredients and mix until smooth. Set aside.
3. To make the batter: In a bowl, with an electric mixer, combine the flour, sugar, baking powder, and salt. On low speed, slowly beat in the butter, egg, and milk until really well blended, up to 2 minutes. Use a spatula to fold in the blueberries.
4. Pour the batter into the prepared pan and spread it into an even layer. Sprinkle the topping evenly over the batter.
5. Bake until a toothpick in the center comes out clean, 45 to 50 minutes.
6. Let cool for 10 minutes. Serve right out of the pan. (Travels well to baseball games if you're in charge of snacks.) You can cut it in squares to serve, but we usually just use a spatula and scoop out as much as we like. It goes great with vanilla ice cream or whipped cream.

ACKNOWLEDGMENTS

When Kathy said, "Let's write a cookbook!" I thought, "Great idea! How hard could writing a cookbook be?"

Now we know: it's hard!

Thankfully, we had help . . . a lot. This project has the fingerprints of dozens of friends and family members on it, and without their help you wouldn't be holding this awesome/amazing cookbook, instead you might be downloading ideas from a Pinterest page, 101 Recipes You Can Bake in a Boot.

Some of the classic Doocy family recipes you'll find in this book originated with friends like Eileen Hansen, Laura Frank, Martha Hockman, Ali Sadri, Susan Ritchie, Goldie Weisz, Joan Keyloun, Mary Vossler, Major Dan, and Jacqy and Sandy Rooney.

Wonderful restaurants and resorts happily shared their dining room classics (and you should visit them whenever you're nearby): Cafe Panache in Ramsey, New Jersey; Sea Island, Georgia; Colonial Williamsburg; Normandy Farm in Blue Bell, Pennsylvania; and Evo Italian in Tequesta, Florida. To professional chefs Paula Deen, Kevin Kohler, and Erik Pettersen: thanks for the private cooking lessons.

Some of our famous friends can now add "cookbook contributor" to their Wikipedia pages: Greg Norman and his mom, Toini; Bob Ritchie and Audrey Berry; Mike Huckabee; Sarah Huckabee Sanders; and Tanya Thicke. Dr. Mehmet and Lisa Oz already have their cookbook credits, so thanks for sharing—just remember, Mehmet, German chocolate cake was *my* favorite before it was *your* favorite (because I am just *slightly* older than you—according to Wikipedia, which is always super reliable).

Then there are the friends who helped us remember timeline details that could have been lost forever; thankfully, their memories helped jog ours: Lea Thompson, the entire Rohde family, Madeline and Todd Van Duren, Bob Brienza, and Tony and Christie deNicola.

My TV family wanted to help and contributed recipes and thoughtful stories: Dana Perino, Martha McCallum, Sean Hannity, Stuart Varney, Toba and Ronni Potosky, Marie Kilmeade (Brian's mom), and Dale Earhardt (Ainsley's mom). Thank you all so much.

Ainsley Earhardt, Brian Kilmeade, Jillian Mele, Janice Dean, Pete Hegseth, Abby Huntsman, and our talented on-air crew—thank you for your kindness, and for ultimately making it easier for me to get up every day before every other single person in the state of New Jersey.

Behind the scenes on *Fox & Friends*: Lauren Petterson, Gavin Hadden IV, Sean Groman, and our wonderful team of producers, bookers, writers, and creative geniuses—thank you for the incredibly hard work and help at my real job. In the Fox

News front offices, big thanks to Suzanne Scott and Jay Wallace. Jaclyn Giuliani, special thanks for coordinating our many media events. To the pre-dawn patrol technical crew of Studio F, you are the best in the business. Don't change anything, except the lighting.

Now to our team at William Morrow, who actually makes books for a living. Lynn Grady, thanks for green-lighting the news guy to cowrite a cookbook. What the hell were you thinking? Kara Zauberman, your amazing attention to detail and assemblage were unparalleled. Jeanne Reina, wonderful art direction for the cover shoot. Tavia Kowalchuk, your marketing plan was ambitious and clever. Anwesha Basu, many thanks for the publicity and precision scheduling and booking us at so many events with wine and cheese.

And an extra special shout-out to Cassie Jones, a gifted editor/writer/mind reader. If we didn't know better, we'd have thought she'd installed a surveillance camera over our range because she always seemed to know what we meant, even when we forgot to write down part of the recipe. Cassie, thanks for guiding us through the world of cookbookery, which is probably not a real word—and Cassie knows it— but she can't edit her own acknowledgment. We don't think . . .

The stunningly beautiful photographs of our recipes are the artwork of Andrew Purcell. He and his team of stylists and kitchen magicians have perfectly captured the exact look we wanted for this cookbook—as if our dishes just popped out of our mothers' ovens.

Tracy Hadden, thanks for making us look adorable on the cover of this book. Michael Crane did a wonderful job taking our wedding pictures on that hot day when the wedding cake melted in the Doocy's car trunk (see page 34). Indian Trail Club of Franklin Lakes, New Jersey—thank you for the beautiful scenery. Sileshi Petro, who worked on book tour logistics—we could not have gotten anywhere without you.

Special note to our literary lawyers, Bob Barnett and Deneen Howell—thank you for your pro bono work on this project. *Ha*—just checking to see if anyone was still reading. Thanks for tending to the legal stuff so we could do the fun stuff.

Finally, to our kids—Peter, Mary, and Sally, the original Doocy family test kitchen—thanks for always being great kids who are now great adults. By the way, Sally took some of our at-home photographs and Mary (the family lawyer) assisted and will probably bill us a couple of quarter hours. #GoodKids.

And to our brothers and sisters and their spouses (and occasional child), who helped with family recipe retrieval and general storytelling—Dub, Rob, Gwen, Cathy, Stephanie, Lisa (and Greg) Ann (and Gus), and Jenny—thanks for helping us remember what dinnertime was like in our homes, back when dishwashers and refrigerators were avocado in color but actual avocados were not available in Kansas.

We love you all. Many thanks and God bless.
Steve and Kathy Doocy

UNIVERSAL CONVERSION CHART

OVEN TEMPERATURE EQUIVALENTS

250°F = 120°C

275°F = 135°C

300°F = 150°C

325°F = 160°C

350°F = 180°C

375°F = 190°C

400°F = 200°C

425°F = 220°C

450°F = 230°C

475°F = 240°C

500°F = 260°C

MEASUREMENT EQUIVALENTS

Measurements should always be level unless directed otherwise.

⅛ teaspoon = 0.5 mL

¼ teaspoon = 1 mL

½ teaspoon = 2 mL

1 teaspoon = 5 mL

1 tablespoon = 3 teaspoons = ½ fluid ounce = 15 mL

2 tablespoons = ⅛ cup = 1 fluid ounce = 30 mL

4 tablespoons = ¼ cup = 2 fluid ounces = 60 mL

5⅓ tablespoons = ⅓ cup = 3 fluid ounces = 80 mL

8 tablespoons = ½ cup = 4 fluid ounces = 120 mL

10⅔ tablespoons = ⅔ cup = 5 fluid ounces = 160 mL

12 tablespoons = ¾ cup = 6 fluid ounces = 180 mL

16 tablespoons = 1 cup = 8 fluid ounces = 240 mL

INDEX

NOTE: Page references in *italics* indicate photographs.

Poultry. *See* Chicken; Turkey
Pumpkin Bourbon Cheesecake, Betty's, *184*, 185

Q

Queen of Cable's Queso, 20

R

Ravioli, Jersey Corn, 84, *119*
Red Pepper Pasta, 136
Red Wine Chicken, 154
Rice, Baked, 158, *159*
Ricotta Board, 21, *22–23*
Ritz Cracker–Breaded Pork Chop, 140, *141*
Rob's Spicy Creamy Deer Pig, *164*, 165
Rocket Chicken, 118, *119*
Roma Tomato Flatbread, 26, *27*
Rub, Mike's BBQ, 157

S

Salads
    Burrata, Tomato, and Pesto, 61, *62–63*
    Fully Loaded Wedge, 66, *67*
    Kathy's California Cobb, 64, *65*
    Potato, Perfect, 72, *73*
    Side, Sally's, 60, *163*
Sally's Grab 'n' Go Bus Breakfast, 39
Sally's Side Salad, 60, *163*
Salmon, Seared, on Avocado Crema, 122, *123*
Sandwiches
    Avocado Toast, 94
    Baby BLT, 91
    Caprese Panini, 95
    Cheesy Bierocks, 92, *93*
    Eggs McDoocy, 40, *41*
    Flaky Ham and Cheese, 98, *99*
    Peter's Chicken Parmesan Sliders, 102, *103*
Sarah Huckabee Sanders's Bourbon Chocolate
    Pecan Pie, 195, *196–97*
Sauces
    Béchamel, *142*, 143–44
    Cheese, 44, *45*

Coffee and Cointreau Cranberry, Kathy's, 172
    Honey-Mustard, *98*, 99
Sausages
    Engagement Lasagna, 111–13, *112*
    Mama Marie's Meatballs, 134–35, *135*
    Queen of Cable's Queso, 20
    Ricotta Board, 21, *22–23*
    Sunday Gravy, 178–80, *179*
    Thanksgiving Dressing, 173
Sea Island Brunswick Stew, 58, *59*
Seared Salmon on Avocado Crema, 122, *123*
Shellfish. *See* Crab
Sides
    Bow Tie Pesto, 82
    Buffalo Hasselback Potatoes, 80, *81*
    Burrata, Tomato, and Pesto Salad, 61, *62–63*
    Dr. Oz's Spiced Mashed Sweet Potatoes with
        Pomegranates, 174, *175*
    Fully Loaded Wedge Salad, 66, *67*
    Green Beans and Goat Cheese, 79, *123*
    Jersey Corn Ravioli, 84, *119*
    Kathy's Coffee and Cointreau Cranberry
        Sauce, 172
    Maple-Bacon Roasted Brussels Sprouts, *74*, 75
    Muffin Pan Potatoes, 85, *147*
    Peanut Butter Pasta, 76
    Perfect Potato Salad, 72, *73*
    Pesto Grilled Corn, 77, *141*
    Peter's Potatoes, 83
    Sally's Side Salad, 60, *163*
    Sweet Potato–Praline Casserole, 78
    Thanksgiving Dressing, 173
Sliders, Peter's Chicken Parmesan, 102, *103*
Smoothie, Steve's 3 A.M. Breakfast, 38
S'mores, Nutella, 216, *217*
Snowball Cookies, Grandma Lil's, 190, *191*
Soups
    Bacon-Corn Chowder, 56
    Fire-Roasted Tomato, and Grilled Cheese
        Croutons, 54, *55*
    Peanut, Peter's, 53

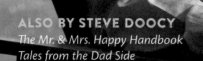

ALSO BY STEVE DOOCY

The Mr. & Mrs. Happy Handbook
Tales from the Dad Side

"King's Arms Tavern Cream of Peanut Soup" developed by John R. Gonzales; from *The Colonial Williamsburg Tavern Cookbook* by The Colonial Williamsburg Foundation, Recipes developed by John R. Gonzales, edited by Charles Pierce, copyright © 2001 by The Colonial Williamsburg Foundation. Used by permission of Clarkson Potter/Publishers, an imprint of the Crown Publishing Group, a division of Penguin Random House LLC. All rights reserved.

"Spiced Mashed Sweet Potatoes with Pomegranate" and "Almost German Chocolate Cake" from *The Oz Family Kitchen: More Than 100 Simple and Delicious Real-Food Recipes from Our Home to Yours by Lisa Oz*, copyright © 2015 by Lisa Oz. Used by permission of Harmony Books, an imprint of the Crown Publishing Group, a division of Penguin Random House LLC. All rights reserved.

Any third party use of this material, outside of this publication, is prohibited. Interested parties must apply directly to Penguin Random House LLC for permission.

FIRST EDITION

Photography by Andrew Purcell, except for pages ii, ix, 232, 234, 236, and 246 by Sally Doocy, wedding photographs on pages 28, 34, 86 and 106 by Michael Crane

Paper texture backgound image by YamabikaY

Library of Congress Cataloging-in-Publication Data has been applied for.

ISBN 978-0-06-283894-0

18 19 20 21 22   LSC   10 9 8 7 6 5 4 3 2 1